MICRO FACTS!

500 FANTASTIC FACTS *about* INVENTIONS

ANNE ROONEY

ARCTURUS

DISCLAIMER

It's great to be an inventor, but not all inventions work very well. Some inventions in this book are old and some are actually dangerous, so don't experiment with copying them! Modern products are tested for safety, so stick with those.

ARCTURUS

This edition published in 2020 by Arcturus Publishing Limited
26/27 Bickels Yard, 151–153 Bermondsey Street,
London SE1 3HA

Author: Anne Rooney
Designer: Sally Bond
Editor: Donna Gregory
Illustrator: Jake McDonald
Supplementary Artworks: Shutterstock

ISBN: 978-1-83857-611-0
CH006560NT
Supplier 43, Date 1019, Print run 8932

Printed in Malaysia

CONTENTS

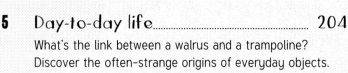

No need to
REINVENT THE WHEEL

Wheels were first made for potters, so that they could whirl their lump of clay around while forming it.

That was 5,500 years ago in Mesopotamia (modern-day Iraq). It took another 300 years for people to realize they could be used to pull chariots.

toy jaguar

In the Americas, wheels weren't used for transport until Europeans arrived. In pre-Columbian America, wheels were added to toys—a wheeled dog, for example—but apparently not used on carts or wagons. That might be because there were no useful animals to pull the carts, like oxen or horses. Try getting a jaguar to pull a chariot …

4

IF YOU'VE GOT JUST ONE WHEEL, YOU CAN MAKE A WHEELBARROW

We don't have any ancient Greek wheelbarrows, but a document listing tools used to build a temple 2,400 years ago includes a "body for a one-wheeler," which can only be a wheelbarrow of some kind.

And that's just what the ancient Greeks did—probably.

The Chinese also invented the wheelbarrow, around 1,900 years ago. One story says army general Jugo Liang invented it to carry heavy loads at the battlefield, and used wheelbarrows as movable barricades. He didn't quite finish the job, though, as he didn't add handles. Another story names a farmer, Ko Yu, as inventor. In either case, the wheelbarrow was kept secret, giving its possessors an advantage.

The first self-powered vehicle was only 65 CM (2 FT) LONG

Flemish missionary Ferdinand Verbiest made the first self-powered vehicle around 1672. He designed and made a steam-powered trolley as a toy for the Chinese emperor.

COOL!

It could run for an hour on one load of coal. Proper steam engines had not been invented, and Verbiest made his own contraption that used coal to boil water, then directed the steam toward a turbine (like a fan), which turned and moved the trolley along.

Because it was so small and not intended to carry people or goods, it doesn't count as a vehicle.

dreadnought wheel

In 1770, Anglo-Irish inventor Richard Lovell Edgeworth suggested "a carriage might be made that should carry a road for itself," but didn't build it. Then in 1846 James Boydell designed the "dreadnought wheel" with solid shoes attached that it "stepped on" in turn, like a caterpillar track for one wheel. It was used on horse-drawn carts and gun carriages in the Crimean War in 1853–6 and on a steam-powered tractor in 1856.

Hornsby paraffin-powered tractor

modern vehicle

In 1858, English inventor John Fowler used a track of eight jointed sections running around a pair of wheels on each side of a vehicle. The English company Hornsby introduced something like the modern caterpillar track in 1905.

NOT SUCH A GOOD IDEA ...

In 1770, Richard Edgeworth proposed a walking wooden horse with eight legs that could step over hedges and fences.

Ever wanted to stand on a helicopter rotor and fly? Best not. The **AEROCYCLE** was scrapped after breaking in test flights in 1956.

American inventor Sylvester H. Roper made a steam-powered bicycle in 1869. The rider had to post lumps of charcoal into a firebox to keep it going.

The **HIGH-BICYCLE**, popular in the 1870s, had a very large wheel at the front and a tiny one at the back. It went fast, and accidents were common.

In 1894, German aviator Otto Lilienthal made an **ORNITHOPTER**—a flying machine with flapping wings. He died in a gliding accident before finishing it.

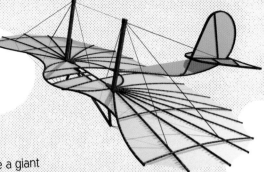

The spherical **VELOCIPEDE** was like a giant hamster wheel for humans. It's hard to see how it's better than just walking …

One-wheeled motorcycles to sit inside have been suggested since the 1930s. One problem is that you can't see where you're going.

The **SINCLAIR C5** was a three-wheeled electric car/bicycle-cross launched in 1985—and scrapped in 1986. Its top speed was 24 km/h (15 mph).

9

Vehicles go best on ROADS

Roads might seem like something that just happened, but they had to be invented and improved over time!

Paths paved with stones or bricks are very old and found around the world. The Romans built roads with large stones underneath and gravel sprinkled on top.

The first roads paved with tar appeared in Baghdad, Iraq, in the eighth century. Tar is made from oil, which is plentiful in the area.

Macadam roads, paved with compressed small stones, were introduced around 1820 by the Scots engineer John Loudon McAdam. The Welsh inventor Edgar Purnell Hooley added tar and sand to the mix in 1902, making Tarmacadam roads that hold together and are waterproof.

Ancient skis preserved in bogs and shown in rock paintings in caves show people had skis at least 5,000 years ago. But they are older than that. Stone Age hunters followed herds of reindeer or elk from Cental Asia using skis wrapped in animal fur, the fur giving them more traction.

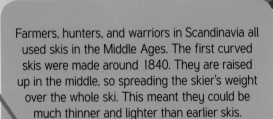

Farmers, hunters, and warriors in Scandinavia all used skis in the Middle Ages. The first curved skis were made around 1840. They are raised up in the middle, so spreading the skier's weight over the whole ski. This meant they could be much thinner and lighter than earlier skis.

Controlled explosions IN A SMALL SPACE are the way to go

The internal combustion engine is at the heart of modern cars.

Robert Street designed the first engine to use liquid fuel in 1794. The French engineers Nicéphore and Claude Niépce built a boat with an internal combustion engine in 1807. The engine was used to power industrial machinery before it was used for cars.

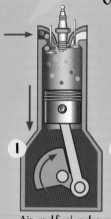

1 Air and fuel under low pressure

2 Air and fuel compressed by moving the piston up

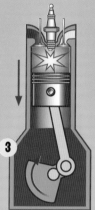

3 Mix ignited by a spark; pressure pushes the piston down

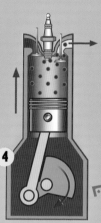

4 Piston pushed up to force waste gases out

The modern four-stroke engine uses a spark to set light to fuel squeezed into a small space. The explosion pushes a piston down, which turns a shaft—a movement that is converted to move wheels or other machinery. The piston moves up to force out the waste gases that are produced by burning the fuel and down to suck in more air and fuel.

A "MAN-MADE FLYING SAUCER" FLOATS OVER THE WAVES

English boat-builder Christopher Cockerell invented the hovercraft—something like a cross between a boat and an aircraft. It floats on an inflated "skirt" that makes a cushion of air underneath the main body. It can go over land or sea, so after crossing water it can ride up a beach.

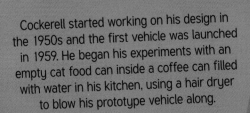

Cockerell started working on his design in the 1950s and the first vehicle was launched in 1959. He began his experiments with an empty cat food can inside a coffee can filled with water in his kitchen, using a hair dryer to blow his prototype vehicle along.

THE CAR CHANGED THE WAY PEOPLE LIVE

Karl Benz combined an internal combustion engine with a chassis in 1885 to make the first car.

Benz's car had two seats, three wheels, and no roof or windows —indeed, no outside at all.

Benz's wife took the car to her mother's house 90 km (56 miles) away. There were a few hitches, but it proved the car was a workable idea.

English inventor, Thomas Parker, built the first electric car in 1884—before Benz's car.

Ferdinand Porsche, made the first hybrid (electric/fuel) car in 1900.

The first mass-market car, the Model T, was launched by Henry Ford in the USA in **1908**.

The Model T was the very first car to be built on a production line.

The earliest sports car was the Prince Henry, made in two models in **1910**.

The first car designed for everyone to own was the Volkswagen Kdf-Wagen released in **1938** in Germany. It could be bought with a special savings scheme.

The Nissan LEAF was the first fully electric car sold, in **2010**.

The Japanese Toyota Prius was the first mass-produced hybrid electric/fuel car in **1997**.

YOU DON'T NEED A NANNY
if you have a GOAT to pull your buggy

The "baby carriage" was invented in 1733 by the English architect William Kent. It was a shell-shaped basket on wheels, low to the ground, that could be pulled by an animal.

Prams—shortened from "perambulators"—soon followed. They were heavy and expensive, made of wood or wicker and metal. At least they were pushed by a person, so families without a spare goat could use one.

modern buggy

The African-American inventor William H. Richardson created the first reversible buggy in 1889. It allowed the baby to face the person pushing. Lightweight buggies came along in the 1960s.

SUBMARINES
WERE PLANNED LONG BEFORE THEY WERE POSSIBLE

The English inventor William Bourne designed a submarine in **1578**, but didn't build it.

Around **1620**, the Dutch inventor Cornelius Drebbel made a modified boat, enclosed in greased leather and powered by oarsmen. His "diving boat" went 4.5 m (15 ft) underwater in the River Thames, London.

More ambitious was Wilhelm Bauer's "sea devil," a wooden submarine powered by crew members working a treadmill to turn a propeller. It made more than 130 dives from **1850** before being lost at sea.

Argonaut

The *Argonaut*, made by American engineer Simon Lake in **1897**, made the first open-sea journey, going from Norfolk, Virginia to Sandy Hook, New Jersey in **1898**. It had a gasoline-powered engine, a periscope, and wheels to trundle along the seabed.

WHEELS GIVE DISABLED PEOPLE INDEPENDENCE

In 1595, the disabled King Philip II of Spain had a chair with small wheels fitted to the bottom of the legs, a rest for his legs, and an adjustable back. His servants could push him around, but he couldn't move it by himself.

A German watchmaker called Stephen Farffler built the first self-propelled wheelchair in 1655. He invented it at the age of 22 because he was paralyzed and couldn't walk.

The first foldable wheelchair was invented in 1923, and electric wheelchairs appeared after World War II to help injured war veterans. The latest developments include a wheelchair that will be able to rise up on two wheels and walk up and down stairs!

An American plumber, Allan Thieme, built the first mobility scooter in 1968 for a relative. Frustrated by the limited options, he wanted to make something that could give his relative proper mobility.

MOBILITY SCOOTERS
are faster than wheelchairs

He built it in his garage— it was bright yellow and could move at 5–6.5 km/h (3–4 mph).

Cheaper than electric wheelchairs, mobility scooters have a handlebar for steering and now whizz along at 12 km/h (8 mph)—but the world record speed for a mobility scooter is 172 km/h (107 mph)!

A boat on stilts goes on top of the water

The hydrofoil was invented by the Italian Inventor Enrico Forlanini in 1906. Alexander Graham Bell, famous for his part in inventing the telephone, built a faster hydrofoil boat in 1919, which held the speed record until the 1960s.

A hydrofoil allows a boat to go on top of the water, reducing drag.

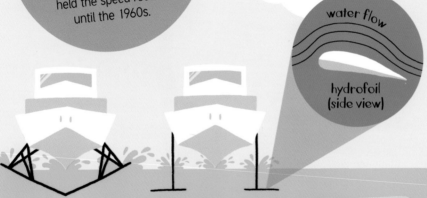

water flow

hydrofoil (side view)

Hydrofoils are planes attached below a boat by struts. At low speeds, the boat is in the water and the hydrofoils are submerged. As the boat goes faster, the hydrofoils create lift and the boat rises off the surface, so just the struts and hydrofoils travel through the water.

The earliest form of elevator was a hoist using a pulley and rope, and dates from at least 2,300 years ago. The Romans even had elevator cages powered by slaves that carried gladiators and wild animals into the arena of the Colisseum in Rome to fight.

GOING UP & DOWN

The first powered elevators used a steam engine. Two English architects designed the "Teagle" elevator in 1835, which had a counterweight to balance the weight of the car going up or down.

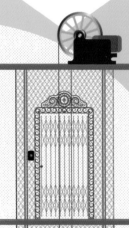

counterweight

The American inventor Elisha Grave Otis designed a safety elevator in 1854 that had self-locking doors to keep passengers safe. His first steam-powered safety elevator was installed in a department store in New York City in 1857.

21

SEGWAYS ARE WHEELY GOOD FUN!

American Dean Kamen invented the Segway in 2001. It has a platform to stand on, two fat wheels beneath, and a handle to hold while the Segway trundles along. Kamen hoped to revolutionize the way that people travel through busy cities. It's half way between being a pedestrian and being in—or on—a vehicle.

A Segway has a system of five gyroscopes to make it self-balancing, so it should be nearly impossible to fall off. Tilt sensors measure position of the weight of the rider 100 times a minute and adjust the Segway's position appropriately.

PUSHING WATER (OR OIL) UPHILL

Many vehicles, including diggers (excavators) and elevators, use hydraulic systems. These work by pushing against a liquid that can't be compressed (squashed).

The principle is simple. Liquid is contained in a closed system of tubes and cylinders with pistons. Pushing the liquid with a piston at one place moves it to another place and so moves one of the other pistons.

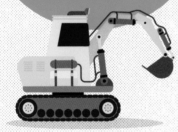

The first hydraulic machine was a printing press made in 1795 by Joseph Bramah. Hydraulics played a key part in the Industrial Revolution of the 1800s. People soon realized oil was a better fluid to use than water as it doesn't damage machinery and can be heated to higher temperatures without boiling.

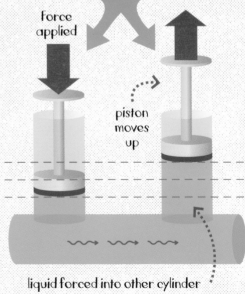

Force applied

piston moves up

liquid forced into other cylinder

DIGGING DEEP

The first diggers or excavators used cables and pulleys to operate the shovel. That changed in 1882 with the first digger to use hydraulics, built by Sir W.G. Armstrong's company in England. It was used to excavate Hull docks. Even this was not fully hydraulic and still had cables and levers. It used water as its hydraulic fluid.

The first fully hydraulic digger was the Direct Acting excavator made by the Kilgore Machine Company in 1897. It had four steam cylinders and used hydraulics to operate all its movements, making it the most versatile digger available—but only five were ever made. Like other excavators at the time, it ran on railway-like tracks.

modern digger

TRAFFIC LIGHTS CAME BEFORE CARS

The first traffic light was built outside the Houses of Parliament in London, England, to control the flow of horse-drawn carriages and pedestrians.

Set up in December 1868, it was operated by a policeman. In the day, horizontal arms stuck out of the side marked "Stop" and "Caution." At night, it used a gas light with red and green lenses. The policeman turned the light round manually, so red faced one way and green the other way—not the most exciting job. Unfortunately, it exploded in January 1869 after less than month.

The first electric traffic light was invented in 1912, and the first with three lights in 1920, both in the USA. Automatic timers were added in 1922.

The BICYCLE was invented because of a VOLCANIC ERUPTION

A volcanic eruption in Indonesia in 1815 led to a very cold summer in Europe in 1816. Among the casualties, many horses starved. The German civil servant Baron Karl von Drais invented a wooden scoot-along bicycle as an alternative to horses. Von Drais covered 13 km (8 miles) in less than an hour on his first trip.

An English inventor, Denis Johnson made a better and very popular version that became known as a "velocipede" or "dandy-horse."

In 1861, a French metalworker Pierre Michaux added pedals to the front wheel, making a recognizable pedal cycle. It was nicknamed "the boneshaker" as it was a rough ride. He started the first bicycle factory in 1868.

THE FIRST CABLE CAR WAS A KINDNESS TO HORSES

Andrew Smith Hallidie invented a ropeway to haul buckets of metal ore across mountains from the mines. He used a loop of constantly moving metal cable to move the load. To make his system stronger, he designed a better metal cable with lots of bendable strands.

When he saw horses struggling to climb the steep hills of San Francisco, he decided to adapt his cable system to make compartments that could move people up and down the hills, sparing the horses. The first cable car railway system opened in 1873.

SWINGING HIGH IN THE SKY

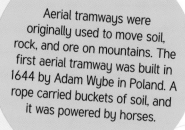

Aerial tramways were originally used to move soil, rock, and ore on mountains. The first aerial tramway was built in 1644 by Adam Wybe in Poland. A rope carried buckets of soil, and it was powered by horses.

In 1893 an aerial tramway in Gibraltar, Spain, was used to carry soldiers along with goods. In the same year, one was also built in Hong Kong to carry workers. It didn't take people long to realize they could be fun and good for sightseeing. The first appeared at Mount Ulia in Spain in 1907.

SELF-DRIVING CARS

The first driverless vehicles were radio controlled or followed wires or tracks on the road. A truly driverless car that can go anywhere only became possible with powerful computers and GPS. In 1994, two robotic vehicles drove 1,000 km (630 miles) on normal roads around Paris at speeds up to 131 km/h (81 mph), but with some human intervention.

A fully driverless bus carried passengers around Schiphol airport in Holland from 1997. A system of magnets buried in the road guided it. Google demonstrated a truly driverless car on open roads in 2015. It carried a legally blind passenger and had no steering wheel or floor pedals.

A kid messing around in a garage invented the snowmobile

When Canadian Joseph-Armand Bombardier was 14, his father got sick of him taking things apart and gave him an old, broken Model T Ford to tinker with in the garage.

One snowy winter, Bombardier built something useful from it. On New Year's Eve 1921, he fitted the motor to two wooden skis and added a propeller from a plane and started it up. He'd invented a snowmobile that could glide over the snow. It took another 14 years before he had a commercial vehicle. He built one for the Canadian Army in World War II, and in 1962 released the Ski-doo snowmobile for fun.

ROCKETS ARE EXTRAVAGANT FIREWORKS

The rockets that carry spacecraft and astronauts into space work in the same way as fireworks, which were invented in China more than 1,000 years ago.

Burning fuel produces energy and waste gases. The waste gases leave the rear of the rocket under pressure, pushing the rocket forward.

The first rocket to use liquid fuel was invented by American engineer Robert Goddard in 1926. It was small and flew to just 12.5 m (41 feet), a flight lasting two seconds.

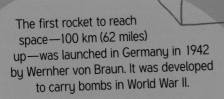

The first rocket to reach space—100 km (62 miles) up—was launched in Germany in 1942 by Wernher von Braun. It was developed to carry bombs in World War II.

Most of a space rocket is thrown away in the FIRST FEW MINUTES

It takes a much more powerful rocket to launch a space vehicle than the small early rockets.

The first rocket used to carry an object into space launched the Soviet satellite Sputnik (see page 98). The rocket provided the fuel and the thrust to get the satellite into the right place, then it was discarded.

multi-stage rocket

The rockets that launched the craft for the Apollo moon landings and later spacecraft are multi-stage rockets. Each stage has its own engine and supply of fuel. After burning its fuel, it separates from the rest and is lost. Goddard designed and patented a multi-stage rocket in 1914 but the first used was the Juno rocket that launched the American satellite Explorer 1 in 1958.

JETS AND ROCKETS ARE THE SAME THING

The first use of any kind of jet engine was around 150 BCE in Roman Egypt. It had a ball that turned as water inside heated and the steam came out of two jets. It wasn't used for anything—it was just amusing.

The jet engine uses this same principle. Air is sucked in through a fan and compressed, then mixed with liquid fuel. The fuel is burned, producing gases that rush out through a nozzle at the back, pushing the vehicle forward.

The jet engine was invented in the 1930s by both Hans von Ohain and Frank Whittle independently. Ohain made the first jet that flew, in 1936.

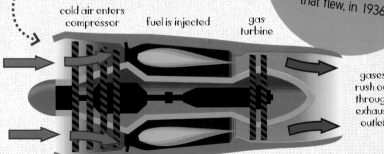

cold air enters compressor

fuel is injected

gas turbine

gases rush out through exhaust outlet

We use sleds now to go over snow. Where wheels would sink in and get bogged down, a sled slides over the top, its weight spread over the runners.

SLEDS were first used on SAND

The earliest known sleds weren't used in snow but in sand. The Ancient Egyptians used curved wooden planks as sleds to move heavy blocks of stone, including statues and obelisks (large columns) over the sand. On dry sand, a sled would get stuck. But by pouring water onto the sand to wet it, Egyptian workers made it easy to haul the sled over the sand.

Bicycles with motors are MOTORCYCLES

Pierre Michaux, who started the first bicycle factory (see page 26), was also the first person to connect a small steam engine to a bicycle to save the rider's legs from the effort of all that pedaling. Others followed suit, but the need to keep adding fuel made it a nuisance.

In 1885, two German inventors, Gottlieb Daimler and Wilhelm Maybach, attached a small combustion engine to a bicycle. They started with the engine. They had just designed it and planned to make a small car to use it, but ended up with the first motorcycle, the Daimler Reitwagen.

Daimler Reitwagen

♥ MOTORS

modern motorcycle

ROLLER-SKATES WERE DANGEROUS FROM THE START

Roller-skates of some kind were used in a stage play in London in **1743**, but no one knows who made them.

The first known inventor of roller-skates was John Joseph Merlin in the **1760**s. He wore them to a party in London, England. He crashed into a mirror, causing himself serious injuries.

Plimpton's four-wheeled skates

A French inventor called Mr Petitbled patented a roller skate in **1819**. it was an in-line skate (with wheels in a single line), but the design made it hard to turn—and stop.

The American inventor James Leonard Plimpton made a four-wheeled skate in **1863** that was much easier to use. He opened the first roller-skate rink in **1866**.

PROPELLERS were used on SUBMARINES before BOATS

The screw propeller has its origins in the Archimedes' screw, designed as a way of lifting water nearly 2,500 years ago. Several people suggested it could be used for moving ships along, starting with the English scientist Robert Hooke in 1683.

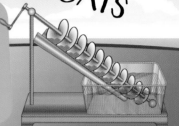

Archimedes screw

Propeller turned by a handle on the inside

The first practical use of a propeller to move a vehicle in water was by David Bushnell on his submarine called the *Turtle*. He built the *Turtle* in 1775, and sailed it underwater to attack *HMS Eagle* in New York Harbor in 1776 during the American War of Independence (unsuccessfully). The Czech-Austrian inventor Josef Ressel used a screw-propellor successfully on a boat in 1826.

THE FIRST HELICOPTER WAS DESIGNED BEFORE THE ENGINE

The principle of a helicopter's whirling blades was copied from seeds that spin in the wind. Chinese children played with spinning bamboo-copters 2,400 years ago. The Italian scientist Leonardo da Vinci drew a vertical take-off "aerial screw" in the 1480s.

Leonardo da Vinci

A French inventor coined the word "helicopter" in 1861 but his own design never took off. The first official helicopter flight was in 1906. French brothers Jacques and Louis Breguet made Gyroplane No.1, which hovered for a minute at a height of 60 cm (2 ft)—but was held by a person at each corner.

The first free helicopter flight came the next year. Paul Cornu's helicopter flew unaided at 30 cm (1 ft) above ground for 20 seconds.

SAFETY FIRST—but good seat belts were a late addition to cars

Wearing a seat belt in a car cuts the risk of death by half. Yet the first cars had no safety belts or very simple belts.

Retractable seat belts for cars were first developed by an American medical doctor, C. Hunter Sheldon, in 1955. Sheldon was distressed by the number of serious head injuries he saw after car crashes and suggested many safety improvements, including roll bars, and even air bags.

The standard three-point rectractable seat belt with a side fastening was designed by Nils Bohlin, an engineer working for Volvo, in 1959. Bohlin realized it had to be really quick to do up and comfortable to wear or people wouldn't use it.

BUGGIES AND ROVERS DON'T GO FAST

Rovers are vehicles that travel over the surface of another planet or the Moon. Some are robotic—they are controlled by computers or from Earth—and others are driven by astronauts.

The first robotic rover was the *Lunokhod I* taken to the Moon by the Soviet *Luna 17* spacecraft in 1970. It covered just 197 m (636 ft) in five days.

The first rover on Mars was Sojourner, which arrived on the planet in 1997.

The Moon buggies were used on the Moon by the American Apollo missions in 1971 and 1972. They were battery operated and driven by astronauts. All three are still on the Moon.

FULL STEAM AHEAD— OVER THE SEA

American inventor John Fitch made the first steamboat in **1787**. It was 13.7 m (45 ft) long and went up and down the Delaware River. In 1807, Robert Fulton launched the first commercial steamboat service, running from New York to Albany, a trip of 241 km (150 miles) that took 32 hours.

These steamboats were paddle steamers and only useable on rivers, but in **1813** Richard Wright launched the first sea-going steamship, a converted wooden boat.

In **1821**, the first specially built iron steamship chugged between England and France.

The first purpose-built transatlantic steamship was launched in **1838**, Isambard Kingdom Brunel's SS *Great Western*.

SOMETIMES A GOOD IDEA COMES TOO EARLY

In 1849, American inventor Alfred Ely Beach suggested a network of underground trains in New York would be a good idea.

Twenty years later, in 1869, he built a tunnel under part of New York, despite not having permission, and installed a pneumatic train system he had designed. (The trains were pushed along by air pressure.)

The tunnel was 95 m (312 ft) long and had only one station (so you had to get back out where you got in, making it pretty useless, if slightly fun).

In the first year, it had 400,000 passengers, but after three years people lost interest and it was closed down.

UNDERGROUND TRAINS GET GOING

The first underground railway system opened in London, England, in **1863**. Passengers sat in open wooden carriages, and the soot and smoke from the steam engine blew all over them. It was dirty, uncomfortable and unhealthy, but 30,000 passengers turned up to try it the day it opened.

The first underground rail system to use electric trains opened in Budapest, Hungary, in **1896**. It ran 3.7 km (2.3 miles) and is still part of the Budapest Metro.

In the USA, Boston was the first city to have an underground stretch of rail, used by streetcars coming into the city in **1897**.

GPS
KNOWS WHERE YOU ARE

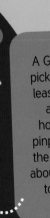

GPS (Global Positioning System) is what tells a satnav where you are. It was designed in 1973 after a group of American military personnel were shut in a room over a weekend and told to stay there until they had come up with a universal navigation system. GPS was the result.

GPS

A GPS receiver works by picking up signals from at least three GPS satellites and, by working out how far it is from each, pinpointing its position on the planet. There are now about 30 satellites devoted to keeping GPS going.

Montgolfier's first balloon

HOT AIR RISES— AND CAN TAKE A BALLOON WITH IT

The Montgolfier brothers Joseph-Michel and Jacques-Étienne were sons of a paper maker. They noticed that trapping heated air inside a paper bag made it rise. They experimented with larger bags, burning wool, and straw to fill their balloons with hot air.

In 1783 they put a rooster, sheep, and duck up in a basket below a balloon. For the duck and rooster it was probably no great adventure, but for the sheep it must have been a surprise.

The balloon landed safely 3.2 km (2 miles) from where it took off after eight minutes. Two months later, they staged a successful flight with human passengers.

45

Driving wheels with HOT WATER

To make wheels turn, a vehicle needs a source of power. A steam engine creates that power by burning coal to boil water to make steam. The pressure of the steam moves a piston, which is attached to the axle of the wheels. As the piston moves, the wheels turn.

steam

boiling water

smoke

piston

burning coal

In **1765**, Scots engineer James Watt made more improvements, enabling the engine to turn wheels. He started making his engines in **1776**.

Steam engines were first made to run stationary machines such as pumps. A Spanish mining administrator, Jerónimo de Ayanz, created a steam-driven machine to pump water from mines in **1606**.

The English engineer Thomas Newcomen made a safer steam engine in **1711**, less prone to exploding.

FLOATING TRAINS USE **MAGNETISM**

Trains run on tracks, right? That's pretty much how we define a train. But **MAGLEV** trains don't move along tracks— they float above them!

weight

magnetic force

A train is slowed down by friction between the wheels and the track, so the best way to get rid of that is to lift the wheels off the track. Maglev trains use electromagnets to keep the train suspended just above the track and to move it forward.

Maglev was invented in 1902 by Alfred Zehden, but there was no way of making such a train then. In 1940, Eric Laithwaite made the first working model engine and the first Maglev train ran in 1984 in Birmingham, England.

FROM TRACKS TO TRAINS

The idea of a "rutway" for wheels cut into rock roads is at least **3–4,000 YEARS OLD**. The wagons were pulled by horses or oxen.

The first railway was a rutway in Ancient Greece **2,600 YEARS AGO**. It was used to drag boats or cargo overland from one part of the sea to another.

In **1803**, the first public railway linked the towns of Croydon and Wandsworth, near London, with carriages pulled by horses.

Tramways with wooden rails were built in England around **1600** to move coal.

In **1768**, some wooden trackways were coated with iron, making iron rails.

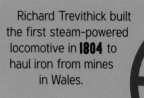

Richard Trevithick built the first steam-powered locomotive in **1804** to haul iron from mines in Wales.

Scots inventor Robert Davidson designed the first electric train in **1837**, but train companies weren't interested until the 1890s.

George Stephenson built his famous steam train *Rocket* in **1829**, setting the design for future stream trains.

Toilets were first added to trains in **1882**, in England.

The first diesel trains were used in **1913** in Sweden.

SURFING ON DRY LAND

The skateboard dates from the 1940s, when it was invented by Californian surfers who were bored when there were no waves to ride. No one knows exactly who started it, but probably the idea cropped up several times independently. It was first called "sidewalk surfing."

The first skateboards were boards with roller-skate wheels attached to the bottom. They developed from kick scooters—a narrow board or beam with wheels, and a wooden crate fixed to the front to act as handlebars for steering. The skateboard was similar, but without the crate and with a wider plank.

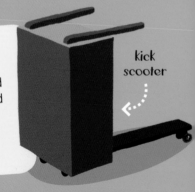

kick scooter

The first two TRACTORS sold were returned to the manufacturer

American farmer John Froelich wasn't happy with the heavy and dangerous steam-powered farm machinery available and decided to make something better.

He created the first tractor in 1892. It was based around an engine powered by gasoline (petrol) and could go both backward and forward.

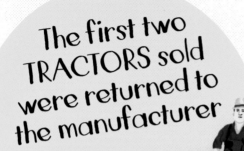

Froelich joined up with some businessmen to make and sell tractors. They sold two, but the people who bought them soon sent them back. The company made stationary machines while working out how to build a better tractor. The better tractor came in 1914, and tractors took off.

modern tractor

51

SKY HIGH

PLANES TAKE OFF

Tito Livio Burattini is said to have built a model aircraft with four fixed glider wings that successfully lifted a cat in **1648**.

English engineer George Cayley made a working model glider in **1804**. It was the first modern heavier-than-air aircraft.

Some time before **1849**, Cayley made a glider that carried a 10-year-old boy, possibly his grandson.

In **1853**, Cayley's full-size glider carried one of his servants on the first properly recorded glider flight.

The American brothers Wilbur and Orville Wright made the first powered flight in **1903** in their *Wright Flyer*. It lasted just a few seconds.

The first passenger plane, or airliner, was the Russian *Ilya Muromets*, which flew with 16 passengers in **1913**. It had a luxurious cabin with a separate lounge and bedroom.

The first working turbojet aircraft was the Heinkel He 178 V1 made in Germany in **1939**.

A plane first broke the sound barrier—went faster than the speed of sound—in **1947** in the USA.

The first human-powered flight across the English Channel was achieved in **1979** by *Gossamer Albatross*, powered by bicycle.

The first stealth plane, Lockheed F-117 Nighthawk, was completed in **1981**. It uses special technologies to hide it from radar.

The first solar-powered plane flew in **2009**. It was produced by two Swiss friends, André Borschberg and Bertrand Piccard.

PAINTING ON THE WALLS

You would get told off for drawing on the walls now, but not in the Stone Age. And just as well—drawings and paintings left on the walls of caves are the earliest forms of communication we know about. They tell us about the lives of the prehistoric people who lived in the caves. The oldest are in Indonesia and at least 40,000 years old. Some in Europe are nearly as old.

Paintings of animals and hunting scenes are precise enough to tell us the types of animals our ancestors lived among. Outlines of hands on cave walls even act like signatures for the individuals who left them.

oldest cave painting, 52–40,000 years ago

handprints, Argentina, 13,000–9,000 years ago

54

PICK UP A PENCIL

The pencil was invented in 1564 near Cumbria in England. People had found large deposits of graphite, a crystallized form of carbon. They made pencils by cutting sheets of graphite into rods and putting them into hand-cut, hollowed wooden rods. They thought the graphite was lead, which is why we still talk of "pencil lead."

In 1795, a French soldier called Nicholas Jacques Conte discovered a way of mixing powdered graphite with clay and making graphite rods. A factory for making pencils opened in 1832, near the English graphite deposits.

The oldest pencil in the world was found in a house built in 1630.

55

A blunt pencil is no good

At first, people sharpened their pencils with a knife. The French mathematician **BERNARD LASSIMONNE** designed the first tool specifically for sharpening pencils in 1828. It had small metal files that you had to rub the pencil against, which sounds like a lot of effort.

The modern portable pencil sharpener has a blade fitted in a conical space where the pencil is turned. That design was created by the French inventor **THIERRY DES ESTIVAUX** in 1849, and you would expect pencil-sharpener inventing would have stopped there. But no.

American **A.B. DICK** designed a mechanical pencil sharpener in 1896, grandly named the "Planetary Pencil Pointer." Two grinding disks rotated and moved around the pencil while the whole contraption was held steady and turned with a crank.

SMILE, PLEASE!

The French inventor Joseph Nicéphore Niépce invented a camera and took the first permanent image with it in 1824. Today, cameras use an exposure of a fraction of a second—Niépce needed an exposure of several days to take his picture of the French landscape.

Niépce's first camera

Luckily, a French painter, Louis Daguerre, worked with Niépce to come up with a better method. In 1839, he revealed the "daguerrotype" process, which preserved images on a thin sheet of copper. Other people soon improved the process—even lifting it from its world of black-and-white with the Lumière brothers' "Autochrome" system in 1907.

57

GOING TO THE MOVIES

It's a short step from still photographs to moving photographs—film! A movie is just a lot of photos shown in quick sequence.

Muybridge's first moving image

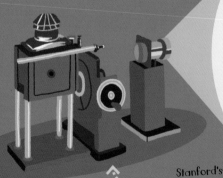

Stanford's projector

The very first movie was made in 1878 to settle a bet between English photographer Eadweard Muybridge and an American businessman, Leland Stanford. Stanford claimed that at some point a galloping horse has all four feet off the ground. Muybridge took a moving film of a horse running, and his 12 frames showed Stanford was right. Stanford helped Muybridge make a projector and they showed the first film in California in 1879.

FROM MOVIES TO TALKIES

Movies soon became a new way of enjoying stories. They had moving pictures, but no sound. Speech had to be shown as frames of text for the audience to read. That rather interrupted the action (and was no good if you couldn't read quickly).

A demonstration of a movie-with-sound took place in Paris, France, in 1900, but the first commercial film with sound was much later—and it only had music and sound effects, no voices! The first "talkie" with recorded voices was *The Jazz Singer* released in 1927.

At first, people thought talkies wouldn't catch on. One movie boss wrote it was **"a good gimmick, but that's all it was."**

"GREAT PARTY, WHAT?!"

"I SHOULD SAY SO"

WRITE IT DOWN

The first society to develop writing was in Mesopotamia (now Iraq) around 5,200 years ago. This first script is called cuneiform. Scribes pressed characters into soft slabs of clay using a specially shaped stick called a stylus. Then they baked the clay to preserve the writing.

cuneiform

Writing also developed in China, about 3,200 years ago. It survives as inscriptions scratched into "oracle bones"— bits of ox bone or turtle shell.

Mayan glyphs

Writing probably began in Central and South America around 2,900 years ago. Everyone thought of it separately, as often happens with a really good idea.

PIECES OF PAPER

Once you have something to write, you need something to write on. Clay tablets are all very well, but they're thick and heavy.

The Ancient Egyptians started using flat sheets of papyrus, made from the stalks of a reed, nearly 5,000 years ago, but paper wasn't invented until just 2,100 years ago.

The Chinese government official Càì Lún was the first person to make paper. He mashed up the bark from mulberry trees and fabric, flattened and squashed the mushy mess, and left it to dry out.

Càì Lún

Paper was better than papyrus as the ink seeped into the paper and couldn't be washed off. That made forging or changing documents hard.

FROM COUNTING TO WRITING

Ten thousand years ago in Mesopotamia, shaped counters stood for common objects.

A cone stood for a basket of grain, an oval stood for a jar of oil.

There were around 300 different tokens —or "words."

After about 4,000 years, people recorded debts by keeping the tokens in a clay "envelope," one for each object.

You can't see what's in a clay envelope without breaking it, so some people pressed shapes into the clay to show what was inside.

Why keep the envelope? They didn't need to. Just a slab of clay would do.

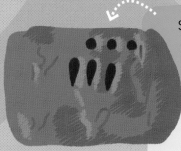

So the first documents were clay tablets listing objects bought, sold, or owed.

Codes for numbers made it easier. Instead of 30 impressions for jars of oil, they used a number followed by the jar symbol.

For example, multiple identical symbols could be swapped to a single symbol for the object and one for a number.

Symbols for sounds—spoken words—appeared 5,000 years ago, first used for names.

ancient name in Sumerian

After names came inscriptions for funerals. It was a written language that could be used for lots of purposes.

63

From stick to pen

The first pens were made of reeds cut with a nib and dipped into ink. They were made in Egypt nearly 2,400 years ago.

People began using feathers in the same way, from about 2,200 years ago right up to the 1800s.

In 1822, John Mitchell started making metal pen nibs in a factory in Birmingham, England, and they soon replaced feathers. A few metal nibs had been made much earlier, even in ancient Egypt, probably for high-ranking officials.

The word "pen-knife" comes from the knife people had to carry to cut down feathers to make pens.

BALLPOINT PENS BY BIRO

In the 1930s, Hungarian journalist László József Bíró wanted a pen that wouldn't smudge. He eventually came up with a design in which the ink flows around a tiny ball in the nib and from there onto the paper. His brother, a chemist, concocted an ink of the right thickness to make it work, and they registered their "Bíró" in 1938.

But then Bíró, who was Jewish, had to flee from the Nazis in Hungary. He ended up in Argentina, from where he got hold of the money he needed to make pens to sell. The first Biros cost the equivalent of about US$43 (£33)!

the nib

SEND ME A POSTCARD!

The first postcard sent in the UK was possibly a joke—and the first sent in the USA was an advert.

The earliest card was sent by English artist Theodore Hook in 1840, to himself. It showed a picture of postal workers that he had drawn. Perhaps he didn't get any letters and wanted one, as the stamped postal system had only just started.

In the USA, the first postcard was sent in 1848. A postcard made good financial sense as the US postal system charged by the number of pages sent and an envelope counted as a page! Sending just a card meant paying for only one page.

POSTCARD

TAP, TAP, TAPPING OUT TELEGRAPHS

needles point to "G"

A
B   D
E   F   G
H   I   K   L
M   N   O   P
R   S   T
V   W
Y

The first automated way of sending a message long distance was the telegraph. It's sent as a electric signals along wires. That means there needed to be wires all over the place for it to work.

William Cooke and Charles Wheatstone built the first telegraph system in Britain in the 1830s. It had six wires, each connected to a needle. All five were needed to send the code for a single character. It was soon used for railway signals—but it needed five wires going everywhere!

In the USA, Samuel Morse worked on a simpler system that used a single wire, so could only send one signal. Then he had to invent Morse code …

DOT, DOT, DASH

When the electrical circuit was completed by the telegraph operator pressing a button, Morse's telegraph sent a signal. At the other end, the receiver made a noise. All that could be varied was how long the operator pressed the button, so Morse devised a code of dots (short presses) and dashes (longer presses).

Each letter was represented by its own set of dots and dashes—S was three dots, E was one dot, T was one dash, and so on.

Common letters had a simple code and ...

less-common letters had a longer, more complicated code.

OVER THE AIRWAVES WITH
WIRELESS

Telegraph needed wires between the places sending and receiving a message. The next step was to go wireless, using radio waves.

The Italian inventor Guglielmo Marconi made the first successful radio transmission in 1894, sending a signal across a room in his house to ring a bell. He proudly showed it to his mother. The next year, he raised the transmitted antenna off the ground and the signal reached up to 3.2 km (2 miles). In 1897 he sent the first transmission over open sea, and the first across the Atlantic in 1901. It wasn't good listening, though—all he transmitted was Morse code.

PRINTING IS OLDER THAN YOU THINK ...

If you have to make each copy of a document with a pen or brush, it's difficult to contact a lot of people at once. Printing made mass communication possible.

The first form of printing began in China about 2,000 years ago. It consisted of rubbing ink onto a carved stone block and pressing paper or cloth against it to take an impression. By 650 CE that had developed to carving text and pictures into a wooden block that could be more easily pressed against paper. Each page had to be hand carved, though lots of copies could be made from it.

MOVABLE TYPE revolutionized PRINTING

Around 1045, Chinese printer **BI SHENG** developed a better system of printing. He made ceramic characters that could be moved around and reused. The characters were arranged in a frame, wiped with ink, and then paper was pressed against them.

The German metal-worker **JOHANNES GUTENBERG** took movable type much further. Around 1450, he made a printing press with a screw device for pressing the paper against the inked type, and developed a better kind of ink. Printed books soon replaced hand-written books. With more books available, more and more people learned to read, changing society for ever.

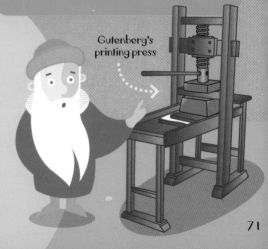

Gutenberg's printing press

Read all about it— NEWS IN NEWSPAPERS

Newspapers could only come about once printing was quick and cheap. The world's first printed newspaper was first issued in what is now Germany in 1609. It was called "Account of all distinguished and commemorable news" (in German, obviously) and was printed by Johan Carolus in Strasbourg.

RELATION: ALLER FÜRNEMMEN UND GEDENCKWÜRDIGEN HISTORIEN

Before this, newssheets were hand written, or people were informed of the news by people who shouted it aloud ("town criers") in a market place or other place where people gathered.

A typewriter prints by pressing metal letters against an ink-soaked ribbon onto paper when the typist presses a key.

TYPING FOR WRITING

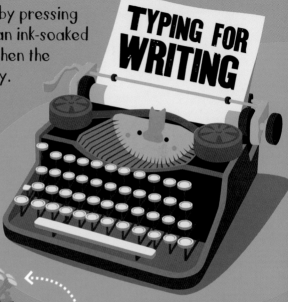

The first typewriter was made in **1808** by the Italian inventor Pellegrino Turri for a blind friend. Letters she wrote on it have survived, but not the machine.

The first successful typewriter was the "writing ball" made in **1870** in Denmark. It was upside-down to our eyes, with the keys on top and the paper underneath.

One with a more modern arrangement was produced in the USA in **1873**. The Sholes & Glidden Type-Writer was pretty, with painted flowers and other decorations. It was replaced in **1878** by the famous Remington 2.

73

From ABC to QWERTY

Have you ever wondered why the keys on your keyboard are in such a strange order? It began in the age of typewriters.

```
2 3 4 5 6 7 8 9 - , —
Q W E R T Y U I O P :
£ A S D F G H J K L M
& Z C X V B N ? ; · !
```

The earliest typewriters had keys arranged A, B, C, D, etc. The first with the letters Q, W, E, R, T, Y starting the top row was the flowery Sholes & Glidden Type-Writer, but it had only capital letters. TYPISTS COULD ONLY SHOUT!

The arrangement of the keyboard we use today was invented by Christopher Sholes, a Milwaukee senator, and newspaper editor. His first try was alphabetical, but the typebars crashed if consecutive letters were used. So Sholes arranged the letters by frequency and combinations of letters to avoid sticking keys.

Word-processing for beginners

With a typewriter, every document has to be typed from scratch and is produced immediately. The process was first automated by storing documents on paper tape, with holes in the tape telling the typewriter which letter to print.

In 1964, IBM introduced a typewriter that used magnetic tape instead. A document stored on magnetic tape could be changed or even deleted and the tape used for a new document. IBM called it a "word-processing machine." Floppy disks were used for storage from 1973.

5 1/4" floppy disk ·······▶

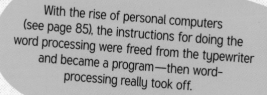

With the rise of personal computers (see page 85), the instructions for doing the word processing were freed from the typewriter and became a program—then word-processing really took off.

THE TRANSISTOR
controlling the flow of electricity

Electronic devices need to make electricity flow where it's needed in the quantity that's needed. The flow is controlled by transistors. They can work as tiny switches, or as amplifiers, taking a small electric signal and making it bigger. In a hearing aid, transistors make a little electric current bigger to make a sound louder.

The transistor was invented in 1947 by three American engineers, William Shockley, John Bardeen, and Walter Brattain.

hearing aid

transistor radio

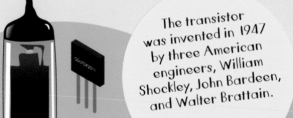

It's much smaller than the vacuum tubes that did similar work before, so electric devices could shrink to more manageable sizes.

vacuum tube

TIME-SLIPPING FOR TELEVISION

In the 1950s, recording a TV program for later broadcast was difficult, so many shows were broadcast live ...

... but that didn't work well in a country like the USA with many time zones, where people weren't watching at the same time. The solution was recordable video tapes.

The first video tape recorder was released in 1956, for TV companies. The first home models came out in 1964, but were too expensive for most people to be able to afford. In the 1970s, three different formats for cheap video cassettes appeared—but someone with one machine couldn't watch tapes made for another. It was a mess that became a war between Betamax (released in 1975) and VHS (1976). Eventually, VHS won.

VHS cassette

video tape recorder

SOUNDS GOOD!

Sound was first recorded and played back with Thomas Edison's "phonograph" in 1877.

The recording was made on foil wrapped around a cylinder. Sound vibrations moved a stylus that traced a line on the foil.

To replay the sound, another stylus followed the line. It was amplified (made louder) through a horn.

In the 1890s, Emile Berliner developed a hard, flat disk with a groove to replace the cylinder—the first record!

In the 1880s, Alexander Graham Bell swapped the foil to a wax-coated cardboard cylinder.

Wind-up gramophones used records, as did later record players.

Magnetic recording began in **1898** with a system of recording onto steel wire. Sounds were converted to electrical signals that magnetized the wire.

Long spools of magnetic tape replaced wires in **1928**.

tape cassette

The first personal cassette player, using plastic magnetic tape in cartridges, was introduced by Philips in **1962**.

1980s personal stereo

Sound recording switched to digital in **1982** with the launch of the first music CDs.

79

Video cassettes were first bought by people to record a TV program to watch later. Soon, film companies started to release films on video cassette.

To avoid the expensive format wars they'd had with the video cassette, all the companies interested in making DVDs got together and agreed the format in advance—a much better way to do things!

Video tapes stretch and if you want to skip to a particular place you have to wind through the physical tape.

The first DVD players were released in Japan in 1996, overcoming both problems. It's possible to skip to any point on a DVD immediately, and, as long as it's not physically damaged, it lasts a long time.

NO MORE DISKS!

Both sound and video went from being recorded on magnetic tapes (or records) to being recorded digitally on flat plastic disks and read by lasers.

But with the development of new file formats, better home computers, and faster broadband internet, people began to buy music and movies just as files to download.

The MP3 file format was developed in Germany, and the record company SubPop released the first MP3 music files in 1999. An MP3 player was released the same year—just as well, as no one wants music files they can't listen to.

Catching the post

WE DEMAND MAIL!

The first mail system was introduced in Persia (now Iran) around 2,500 years ago. The king (either Cyrus the Great or Darius I) demanded that every province have a system that could collect and deliver mail from every citizen.

Darius I

Cyrus the Great

The first well-documented service ran in ancient Rome 2,000 years ago. It even had postal carriages pulled by fast horses.

There were early postal systems in India, China, and Mongolia, too. By 1294, the Mongolian Empire had a postal service with 1,400 postal stations just in China, with 4,000 carts, 6,000 boats, and 50,000 horses. And 1,150 sheep ... letters delivered by sheep?

STAMPED MAIL IS PAID FOR IN ADVANCE

Before the introduction of the stamp in England in 1840, postage was paid for by the person who received the letter. How much it cost depended on how many sheets of paper were sent and how far the letter was carried. So a quick note on one sheet to the next village was cheap, but a long document sent between cities cost a lot.

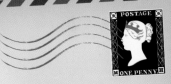

The first stamp was called a Penny Black because it was black and cost one penny. Not very imaginative, is it? It was suggested by Rowland Hill. With the first sticky stamp and pre-paid postage, it marked the start of the first modern postal system.

DOES NOT COMPUTE— OH, YES IT DOES!

Charles Babbage designed the first computer, his **DIFFERENCE ENGINE**, in **1822**, but didn't build it.

A working Difference Engine was built at the Science Museum, London, in 1991 (see page 86).

The first working computer was **COLOSSUS**, made in secret in England during World War II to crack German army codes.

Colossus was destroyed after the war as it was an official war secret!

The first multi-purpose programmable computer was **ENIAC**, built in the USA in **1945**.

The first computer that could store programs was called **BABY** and made in Manchester, England, in **1948**.

The first computer to use a desktop, menus and icons was the **XEROX ALTO**, launched in **1973**.

The Altair 8800 was the first personal computer, launched in **1975**. The user had to build it from a box of bits.

The Altair had no keyboard, no screen, no mouse, no way of storing programs, and no printer.

The first removable storage for personal computers was cassette tapes, the same as those used for audio.

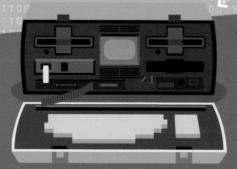

The first portable computer was much bigger than a laptop—the Osborne I weighed 10.7 kg (24.5 lb)! It launched in **1981**.

ADA'S LANGUAGE

Difference Engine

The very first computer programming language was written by Ada Lovelace, a friend of Charles Babbage who *didn't* build the first computer. Ada was a talented mathematician, and worked out the instructions that Babbage's Difference Engine would follow if he built it. A computer language has been named after her, called "**ADA.**"

The first computer language actually used was called **SHORT CODE** and appeared in 1949. The programmer had to convert the instructions to 0s and 1s for the computer to understand (a task called "compiling" which is now done automatically). The first major computing language developed was **FORTRAN** in 1957, designed for scientific computing.

Moving pictures at home

The first demonstration of a working television took place in the fancy London department store Selfridge's in 1926.

The Scots engineer John Logie Baird invented it. He took the principle of sending sound through the air carried as radio waves and extended it to carrying images in the same way.

A TV with nothing to watch is not much use. The first electronic television service started in Berlin, Germany, in 1935. The British Broadcasting Corporation (BBC) began a regular broadcasting service in 1936.

The first broadcasts were in black and white, but from the 1950s screens used red, green, and blue pixels, to show lots of different hues and tones.

READING WITH YOUR FINGERTIPS!

Most writing is flat on the page, so blind people can't read it. Luckily, there is an alphabet for people who can't see— they read it with their fingertips.

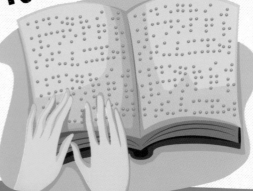

BRAILLE is a code of raised dots arranged into patterns to stand for letters. It was invented in 1824 by Louis Braille, a 15-year-old French student blinded in childhood. In 1829, Louis Braille extended his system to include musical notation, so blind people could read music, too.

The first machine for writing Braille was the Hall Braille writer, invented in 1892 by Frank H. Hall, who worked at the Illinois School for the Blind.

WIRES DON'T NEED TO BE WIRED — THEY CAN BE PRINTED

The printed circuit board (PCB) miniaturized electrical circuits. Instead of a base-board with wires, lines are printed in copper onto an insulating board and other components connected to these lines, which act as wires. The insulating board is first covered with a layer of copper foil, then with an etching solution, then an image of the circuitry is projected onto it from a light source. The solution eats away the copper everywhere except where "wires" are needed.

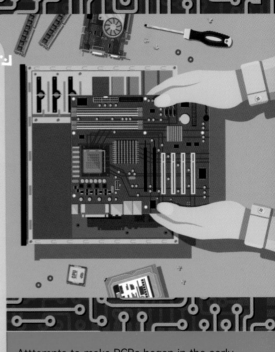

Atttempts to make PCBs began in the early 1900s, but the first actual PCB was made by the Austrian engineer Paul Eisler, working in England on radio sets around 1936.

Making everything SMALLER made everything possible

All modern electronics depend on **MICROCHIPS**, which are also called integrated circuits or silicon chips. These are rather like miniaturized printed circuit boards (PCBs). Instead of the circuitry being printed in the form of wiring and other components being added to an insulated board, the entire circuit and all its parts are reduced to an etched wafer of silicon (a semi-conducting material).

The microchip was invented by American engineers Jack Kilby and Robert Noyce in 1959.

Now microchips are in everything from your smartphone to programmable washing machines, watches, cars, and even singing birthday cards. They can pack billions of transistors and other circuitry into a tiny area, so all electronic devices can be miniaturized.

83KFH-83

KL293-12
9-3-20

THE FIRST MOUSE WAS WOODEN

The computer mouse was invented by Douglas Engelbart in 1964 and demonstrated four years later in 1968. In his presentation, Engelbart described using windows, hyperlinks, networked computers, and a mouse so that people could share information and work together. The worldwide web still lay more than 20 years in the future and no computers had a system of windows, icons, and menus.

Engelbart's mouse was made of wood and had wheels underneath. It connected to the computer with a cable.

The first personal computer to be shipped with a mouse was the Apple Lisa in 1983. The mouse became popular after the first Apple Macintosh computer was released in 1984.

hello.

the first Apple Macintosh with mouse!

91

Julius Caesar might have invented the notebook

Ancient Romans used a set of wooden tablets each covered with wax that could be written on by scratching with a stylus.

Around 1900–2000 years ago, someone—possibly the emperor, Julius Caesar—had the idea of replacing the wooden tablets with sheets of parchment (animal hide used as paper) bound together. So the book format, or "codex," seems to have come from writing rather than reading.

Before books, texts were presented as scrolls—long single sheets that were stored rolled up. When books came along, they soon took over. They're easier to use and store and cheaper, as they use both sides of the paper or parchment.

STORIES ON SCREEN

Do you like to read on paper or on a screen?

"E-ink" and "electronic paper" mimic the appearance of print on paper, but on a screen. They were introduced in 1997, and the next year brought the first ebook reader, the Rocket eBook. People weren't convinced it was a good idea until the Sony Reader came out in 2006. Then when Amazon introduced the Kindle in 2007, it sold out in just over five hours.

For a few years, e-book readers were very popular, but soon general-purpose tablets and smartphones appeared. Dedicated e-book readers became less popular. Who knows what you will be reading from in 20 years' time?

COMPUTERS TALK TO EACH OTHER

There were no kitten videos or memes at the start of the internet. It was all dreary-looking text, most of it about science and engineering.

In 1962, J.C.R. Licklider described a "Galactic Network" of linked computers all over the world to communicate and share information. That's pretty much what the internet has become.

It got going in 1969 as "**ARPANET**," linking computers in four American universities. It worked by chopping information into small packets and sending them by different routes over the telephone network, then putting the information back into the right order—just as it does now.

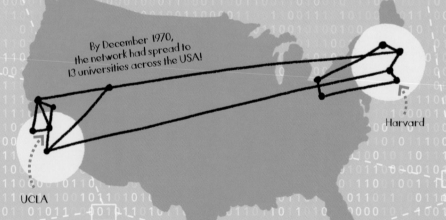

By December 1970, the network had spread to 13 universities across the USA!

Harvard

UCLA

Email made **SPAM** possible ...

The "killer app" that led to the internet really taking off in 1972 was the invention of a simple electronic text messaging service. It was invented by Ray Tomlinson in the USA and became the email systems we have today.

Tomlinson's system allowed people to send messages between computers. He chose the @ symbol to separate the name of the person (the username) from the name of the host computer system, giving us the format of **NAME@ORGANIZATION** for email addresses that is still used.

The first spam email was sent in 1978. It was an advertisement for a presentation about a new computer, sent to 400 of the 2,600 people on ARPAnet.

WEAVING THE WEB

Twenty years after ARPANET started, British scientist **TIM BERNERS-LEE** thought of making linked text to connect documents on different computers using the internet. He suggested what is now the world wide web to his boss, who said the idea was too vague and didn't give him money to develop it.

Luckily, Berners-Lee was enthusiastic and did it anyway. He designed HTML (hypertext mark-up language), the principle of web addresses, a means of moving information around, and the first web browser (so that the pages could be displayed). He demonstrated them in 1990.

He made it free and open for everyone to use, which it still is. So **NOW** we can have kitten videos and memes.

96

PUT IT IN AN ENVELOPE ...

Unless it IS the envelope!

The first commercially produced envelopes were actually lettersheets—pieces of paper you wrote on and then folded to make an envelope that could be sealed with sealing wax.

When the British postal service launched in 1840, it did so with the sale of "Mulready" lettersheets, which had a design on the outside and came with pre-paid postage of one penny (the cost of a stamp). This was an alternative to buying a separate stamp. The design was so fancy it was widely mocked, and people thought it showed the government was trying to control the supply of envelopes. Most people used plain envelopes and bought stamps.

lettersheet unfolded

folded

97

SATELLITES GO ROUND AND ROUND AND ROUND

Satellites are objects that go around Earth (or sometimes the Sun) in space.

They have lots of uses, from telecommunications and weather to providing GPS services and carrying telescopes.

The fist satellite ever launched was the Soviet **SPUTNIK** in October 1957. A larger satellite had been planned, but problems led to the launch of a much smaller one to prove it was possible, and to get into space before any American missions.

Sputnik was the size of a beach ball at 58 cm (23 in) across and weighed 83 kg (184 lbs). It sent radio signals to Earth for 22 days and burned up in Earth's atmosphere after two months.

GOING ROUND or STANDING STILL?

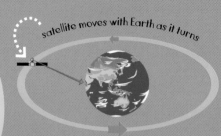

satellite moves with Earth as it turns

Geostationary satellites are a special type of satellite and a vital part of communications networks on Earth. They stay above the same spot on Earth all the time—but not by standing still, as Earth moves underneath them. A geostationary satellite orbits Earth exactly once every 24 hours, moving with Earth as it turns.

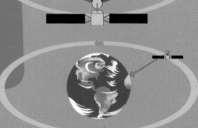

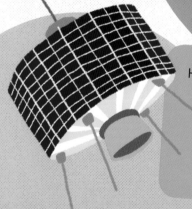

Harold Rosen invented the first geostationary satellite, **SYNCOM 2**, launched in 1963, but the idea was first suggested in 1928. The first working communications satellite, Syncom 3, was used to broadcast the Olympic Games from Tokyo to the USA in 1964.

RING, RING

Two inventors, Alexander Graham Bell and Elisha Gray, both invented the telephone at the same time.

Bell was trying to improve the telegraph when he came up with the better idea of transmitting human voices through wires.

They registered their designs with the US patent office within hours of each other in **1876**—Bell was first.

The first permanent outdoor phone wire was set up in 1877. It was just 4.8 km (3 miles) long.

The first telephone exchange opened in **1878**. All calls had to be connected by an operator.

Telephone numbers were introduced in **1879**. Before that, people just gave the name of the person they wanted to be connected to.

The first automatic dialing system arrived in **1891**.

The first coin-operated phone was installed in Hartford, Connecticut, USA, in **1889**.

By **1918**, there were 10 million phones in the USA.

The first transatlantic phone transmissions, in **1927**, went by radio.

Laying transatlantic phone lines under the sea began in **1955**.

101

TOUCHY-FEELY SCREENS

We use touchscreens every day, on phones, tablets, and laptops, in stores, libraries, and schools.

The touchscreen was invented in **1965** by a British radar engineer, E.A. Johnson. His design of pressure touchscreen was used by air traffic control systems until the late 1990s.

Resistive touchscreens (which respond to a finger or a stylus) were invented in **1970**. Physics researchers using electrically conductive paper in their research realized that they could convert it to a screen with electrical wires on two layers that completed a circuit—and registered a location—when pressed together.

HP released one of the first touchscreen computers in **1983**, and the first touchscreen phone followed in **1993**.

The first mobile telephone network began in 1946, connecting phones in vehicles with a telephone network by radio. Each call was connected by an operator and there were only a few radio channels, so few people could make calls at the same time in each city!

The first SMARTPHONE was called SIMON

In 1973, Motorola showed the first handheld mobile (or cell) phone. Never mind that it cost nearly US$4,000 and the battery took 10 hours to recharge and only lasted 30 minutes—people were excited! The first cell phone network began in Japan in 1979.

The first smartphone was the IBM Simon, launched in 1993. It had lots of apps and a screen with a stylus, but wasn't connected to the internet—that came along in Japan in 1999.

103

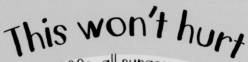

This won't hurt a bit

Until the 1800s, all surgery was incredibly painful. And if you had an accident, there was no way to stop your injury hurting.

Then in 1789, English scientist Humphry Davy discovered that the gas **NITROUS OXIDE** made him laugh and numbed pain. He didn't do anything useful, though, like encourage doctors to use it.

inhaling nitrous oxide from an animal bladder

At last, in 1845, it was used to put a patient to sleep for an operation. Unfortunately, the patient woke up part way through. The next year, a different chemical, ether, was used. It seemed like a miracle—people could suddenly have teeth pulled and broken bones set without feeling a thing.

BREATHE IN, BREATHE OUT

The Scottish doctor James Young Simpson discovered in 1847 that **CHLOROFORM** was even better than ether as an anesthetic. Chloroform is a liquid, and it had to be breathed in as a gas—but it couldn't just float around the operating room as the medical staff would also fall asleep. Putting a cloth soaked in chloroform over a patient's face worked, but some of the chloroform escaped into the room.

The English doctor John Snow invented an inhaler to give chloroform just to the patient. It had a face mask attached by a tube to a flask of chloroform. Chloroform became very popular after the Queen Victoria used it during childbirth in 1853.

$CHCl_3$

ZZZZ

JUST A LITTLE NUMB

Chloroform was fine if a doctor needed a patient to go to sleep, but sometimes an operation is only on a small part of someone, so being fully unconscious is not necessary.

After a girl died from chloroform use during a very minor operation on a toe, people started to look for local anesthetics—medicines that would numb just part of the body while the patient stayed awake.

The first local anesthetic was cocaine, first used as a medicine in Germany in 1884. The Incas in ancient Peru used leaves of the coca plant for centuries. Because it was very addictive, it was replaced in 1903 by less dangerous forms of the same medicine.

coca leaves

IT'S JUST A SCRATCH

Mrs. Dickinson was very accident prone. In 1920, her husband Earle came up with the idea of getting dressings ready *before* she had an accident.

He worked for a medical supplies company, called Johnson and Johnson, and had a ready supply of surgical sticky tape and gauze (a light fabric used for covering wounds). He began to cut strips of tape and put a piece of gauze on them so that she could easily stick them over any cuts and scratches.

BAND-AID

Dickinson's employer soon turned his idea into a commercial product. The first sticking plasters went on sale in America in 1924.

107

Put your best (FAKE) foot forward

People who lose a limb, or are born with one missing, often use a fake limb, called a prosthetic. The oldest surviving prosthetic is a wooden toe from Ancient Egypt.

Toes are very important—it's difficult to balance to walk properly without a big toe. The wooden big toe was made 3,000 years ago for the daughter of a priest. It attached to the woman's foot with a leather strap. It both worked as a toe and looked realistic.

As Egyptians wore open-toed sandals, looking realistic probably mattered a lot to her.

CLEAR-SIGHTED

The first eye-glasses or spectacles were made in the 1200s by an Italian called Salvino D'Armate. He told an Italian monk, Allesandro della Spina, who told everyone else—and possibly pretended he had invented them.

The first glasses had frames made of bone or metal, and lenses made of quartz, a see-through stone. They were convex (bulging outward) and helped people who were far-sighted.

concave lens

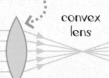

convex lens

In 1451 Nicholas of Cusa, a German glassmaker, made concave lenses (dipping inward in the middle) to help people who were short-sighted.

Early spectacles had to be held in place or balanced. The British optician Edward Scarlett added arms at the side to hook over the ears in 1727.

ONE IN THE EYE

English physicist Thomas Young tried to make contact lenses in 1801. They must have been uncomfortable. They consisted of a glass tube just 6 mm (¼ in) long filled with water. He glued them to the surface of his eyeballs with wax. Seriously. Not surprisingly, he couldn't see any better with them than without them.

Adolf Fick made slightly better lenses in 1888, but they weren't great. They covered the entire eye and were made of heavy glass. Wearers suffered terrible eye pain after just a few hours.

SCRIVENS LTD.
LONDON & MIDLANDS

The first plastic lenses also covered the eye, in the 1930s. Then in 1948 Kevin Touhy accidentally broke a lens he was preparing. He tried out the small lens and found it still worked!

Thermometers were first made for measuring the temperature of the air.

Taking a patient's temperature helps a doctor work out what is wrong with them.

FEELING HOT?

The first doctor to use a thermometer with his patients was Herman Boerhaave, in the **1860**s. It took a long time to take a patient's temperature— about 20 minutes—and the thermometer was 30 cm (1 ft) long! (It went in the patient's armpit.)

The first thermometer for putting in a patient's ear was invented in **1964**.

Thomas Albutt invented a clinical (medical) thermometer in **1866** that really speeded things up, as it showed a patient's temperature in just five minutes.

A stitch in time ...

Large cuts and wounds are often stitched together to help them heal. The stitches are called "sutures."

The first sutures were used in Ancient Egypt about 5,000 years ago. They were made of plant material such as hemp or cotton, or animal matter including "catgut," which is actually made from sheep intestines, not cat.

In some places, people used ants to suture wounds! They got the ants to bite through the sides of the wounds, holding them together, then snapped off the body, leaving the jaws as a suture.

No one sterilized the material used for sutures until the 1860s, so they must have introduced a lot of germs to the body.

112

A DROP OF BLOOD

If people lose a lot of blood in an accident they might need a blood transfusion. This is blood given by someone else.

In 1655, British doctor Richard Lower first successfully moved blood from one dog to another. From 1667, people tried moving blood from animals to humans but it was soon banned as people became sick. The first successful human blood transfusion was carried out by Philip Syng Physick, in America in 1795.

transfusion from a lamb

Sometimes blood transfusions worked and sometimes they went badly wrong. They only became safe after the discovery of different types of blood in 1900 and the realization in 1907 that people must be given compatible blood.

O
A   B
AB

compatible blood types

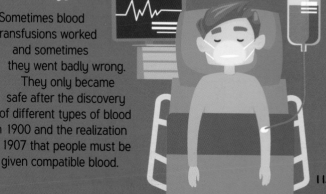

113

HELP WITH BREATHING

Today lots of people rely on asthma inhalers to help their breathing.

The first type of inhaler was invented in England by John Mudge in 1778. It was an adapted tankard (a metal drinking mug) that he used to breathe in medicine to treat a cough.

Pressurized inhalers were invented in 1955 by American doctor George Maison. His daughter had asthma, and struggled to breathe in enough vaporized medicine. He realized a medicine that forces the right dose of medicine into the lungs under pressure would make life much easier for her—and for millions of other people.

CHOMP, CHOMP

False teeth have been around for 2,700 years, but originally they were not actually fake—just other teeth put into the patient's mouth. Sometimes they were animal teeth, or teeth from a dead person. And sometimes they were even the owner's original teeth, fixed back in with wires!

The first truly false teeth were made in Japan in the early 1500s. They were carefully carved from wood and fixed to beeswax fitted to the patient's mouth.

Later, Japanese dentists—and then others elsewhere—used teeth carved from bone, human teeth or animal teeth. American President George Washington had a set of teeth carved from hippopotamus and elephant ivory. The first porcelain teeth were made in 1770.

George Washington

JUST TAKE A PILL

Aspirin is the most used medicine in the world. It's main ingredient, salicylic acid, was extracted in **1829**.

willow tree

Salicylic acid is found in willow trees. People first used willow bark as a medicine at least **4,000 YEARS AGO**.

Ibuprofen was made in **1961** and first sold as a painkiller in **1969**.

Paracetamol was first made in **1878**, but medicines containing it didn't become common until the **1950S**.

The statins that people take to prevent heart attacks were introduced in **1978**.

The MMR triple vaccine to prevent measles, mumps and rubella was invented in **1971**.

The first vitamin pills were introduced in **1934** in Switzerland. They provided vitamin C.

Penicillin, the first antibiotic, was first used in **1942**.

The asthma inhaler Ventolin was introduced in **1969**.

Children's medicine Calpol was introduced in **1966**.

The first antihistamine medicine to treat allergies was launched in **1942**.

CALPOL

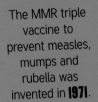

117

LENDING AN EAR

An "ear trumpet" captures sound and funnels it into the ear. It works just by having a larger opening than the ear does. The first ear trumpets were hollowed out animal horns used in the 1200s, and artificial ones appeared in the 1700s.

Ear trumpets don't actually amplify (magnify) sounds. That began with the first electric hearing aids, invented in 1902 using technology developed for the telephone.

At first, electric hearing aids were huge and heavy, and not portable. The first wearable hearing aids came in 1952 with the invention of the transistor (see page 76).

In the LOOP

You might have seen—or used—the "hearing loop" system offered in some public places to make life easier for people who can't hear well.

$X+y=$

The induction loop system was invented in Britain by Joseph Poliakoff in 1937, and the first hearing aids that could use it appeared the year after.

A microphone or a sound source such as TV is connected to an amplifier, which connects to a loop of wire running around a room. Sounds are magnified and travel through the wire loop. A user's hearing aid picks up loop signals and it converts them back to sounds.

Listen to your heart

A stethoscope lets a doctor or nurse listen to sounds in your body, such as your heartbeat or breathing.

René Laennec made the first stethoscope in France in 1816. It was nothing like the modern stethoscope. Laennec's stethoscope was a simple tube. He put one end against the patient's body and the other to his ear. He invented it because he felt uncomfortable putting his ear directly on the chest of female patients.

In 1840, Golding Bird designed a stethoscope with a flexible tube, and in 1851 Irish doctor Arthur Leared added two earpieces. The familiar style of stethoscope went on sale the following year.

SEEING INSIDE WITH MAGNETISM

Did you know doctors can see inside your body using magnets?

Magnetic resonance was discovered in 1946 but not used in medicine until 1971. Normal body tissues and cancerous lumps change briefly when exposed to a strong magnetic field, and return to normal at different rates. By measuring how tissues in the body behave, it's possible to work out which areas are normal and which have abnormal growths that could be cancers.

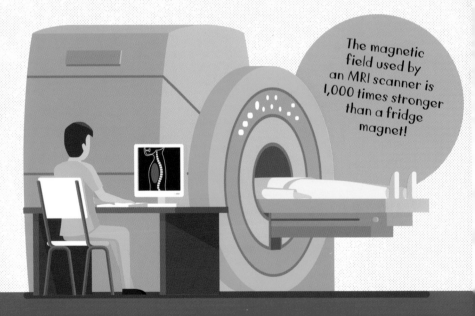

The magnetic field used by an MRI scanner is 1,000 times stronger than a fridge magnet!

MRI scans are now a valuable way of checking whether someone has cancer.

SEEING INSIDE WITH X-RAYS

If you've ever broken a bone, you've probably had an X-ray.

X-rays were discovered by the German chemist Wilhelm Roentgen in 1895. He found he could use them to "see" through lots of soft substances, and cast a shadow of more solid objects. He made the first anatomical X-ray—of his wife's hand, complete with her wedding ring.

Within just a month of his discovery, people were using X-rays to look inside bodies. They were soon used on battlefields to find bullets inside the bodies of injured soldiers.

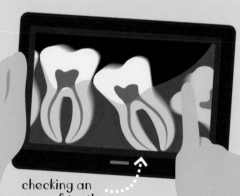

checking an x-ray of teeth

SEEING INSIDE WITH SOUND

Ultrasound works by sending out very high-pitched sounds and then "listening" with a machine for the echoes that bounce back and using them to make an image. It can be used for things like mapping the seabed—and also for looking inside bodies.

Ultrasound was first used medically in 1956 in Scotland, but didn't really take off until the 1970s. It's commonly used to look at unborn babies to make sure they are growing properly. Before ultrasound scans, people just had to hope for the best and wait for the baby to be born.

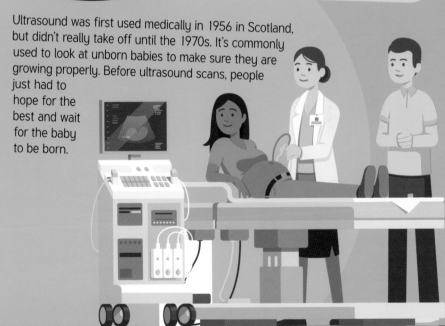

SEEING INSIDE WITH A TUBE

If a doctor wants to check inside your gut, they can use an endoscope—a long bendy tube with a camera at the end.

Adolph Kussmaul made the first endoscope in Germany in **1868**. He tested it on a sword-swallower who could swallow the rigid tube, 47 cm (41 in) long and 1.3 cm (0.5 in) across. Not many patients are sword-swallowers, though, so its use was limited.

A thinner, but still rigid, version appeared in **1881**. The first bendy endoscope was developed in **1932**.

The real breakthrough came in **1964** with a new material—very thin strands of glass. Using them in an endoscope fitted with a camera allowed doctors to see and photograph right inside a body.

124

Tiny holes for BIG OPERATIONS

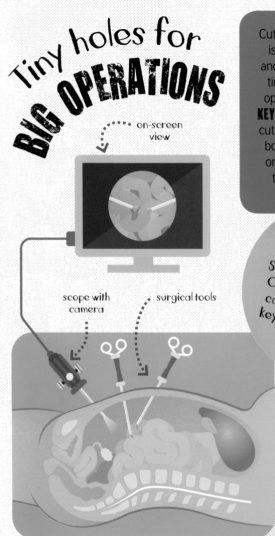

on-screen view

scope with camera

surgical tools

Cutting a big hole in someone is not very good for them, and a big wound takes a long time to heal. Instead, some operations are now done by **KEYHOLE** surgery. The surgeon cuts several small holes in the body, puts an **ENDOSCOPE** in one and uses small surgical tools through the others.

The first attempt was on a dog in 1901. The Swedish doctor Hans Christian Jacobaeus carried out the first keyhole surgery on a human in 1910.

In the 1970s, computerized television cameras were invented. They could project an image from inside the body on a screen. That made keyhole surgery much easier and it became widely used.

A heartbeat away

A pacemaker regulates a person's heartbeat if their heart can't do it reliably. Pacemakers trigger the heart muscle to contract (the heart to "beat") with an electric current.

An Australian doctor produced an early pacemaker in 1926 that plugged into mains electricity. In 1928, it revived a baby whose heart wasn't beating when it was born. But then research stopped as people made a fuss about "reviving the dead."

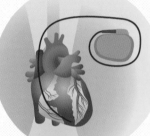

modern pacemaker

Although a Colombian team made a pacemaker powered by a car battery in the 1950s, it was still too large to carry around. The first wearable pacemaker was designed in the USA in 1958. Modern pacemakers are fitted inside the chest and are completely unnoticeable.

first wearable pacemaker 1958

SMALLPOX, COWPOX, OR NO POX?

Smallpox is a terrible disease that killed millions of people before it was wiped out by vaccination in 1979. It was the disease for which vaccination was first invented.

In China, 1,000 years ago, people crushed up scabs from smallpox spots and blew the powder into the noses of healthy people. The patients usually developed a mild case of smallpox and were then immune for the rest of their lives.

An English doctor, Edward Jenner, made the process safer and carried out the first vaccination in 1796. He noticed that people with cowpox sores never caught smallpox. Cowpox is a mild disease, and never deadly. Jenner used gunge from the sores of milkmaids with cowpox to make a vaccine against smallpox.

A HELPING HAND (OR LEG)

The oldest artificial leg was found in Italy. It was made **2,300 YEARS AGO** from bronze and iron.

A Roman writer described an army general who lost an arm **2,200 YEARS AGO** and had a metal one made that could hold a shield.

In the **1500S**, French doctor Ambroise Paré made a hinged mechanical hand and prosthetic legs with a locking knee.

In **1812** a false arm was invented that could be controlled by the opposite shoulder, using connecting straps.

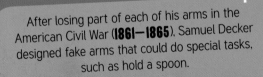

After losing part of each of his arms in the American Civil War (**1861—1865**), Samuel Decker designed fake arms that could do special tasks, such as hold a spoon.

In **1946**, after World War II produced many casualties, a suction sock was developed for attaching false legs.

In **1960**, the Russian scientist Alexander Kobrinski made the first myoelectric limb. Signals from the person's muscles are picked up by electrodes on the skin to control it.

In **1984**, engineer Van Phillips invented the running blade, prosthetic legs designed for running. They don't look like natural legs.

In **2018**, a man who lost an arm was fitted with the first prosthetic arm that is controlled by thought.

Cutting people open—SAFELY

Until the middle of the 1800s, operations were extremely dangerous and painful. Then with the use of ether they became tolerable, but were still dangerous. Many patients died of infections.

That changed in 1865 when the Scots surgeon Joseph Lister had the idea of using a spray of **CARBOLIC ACID** in the operating theatre.

Carbolic acid is an antiseptic. It kills germs that cause wounds to become infected. Lister had already started using dressings soaked in carbolic and encouraging surgeons to wash their hands and wear clean clothes.

It seems crazy now that doctors didn't bother about being dirty when they carried out operations!

130

NEEDLES ARE NICE—

or nicer than they used to be!

The hypodermic needle was invented in 1844 by the Irish doctor Francis Rynd.

The needle was too thick to pierce the skin, so the doctor cut a hole in the skin with a blade, put in a tube, and then put in the medicine. How horrible would that be?!

The first needle fine enough to pierce skin was developed in 1853.

The syringe itself had been around a long time. The Romans used piston syringes to deliver medicines nearly 2,000 years ago. And Native Americans made a kind of hypodermic using hollow animal bones for the needle and small animal bladders like a syringe to hold the medicine. It sounds quite unhygienic.

modern syringe

From ACCIDENT to INVENTION

Don't like needles? A jet injector forces a medicine against the skin at such high pressure that it goes through without a needle.

skin

jet injector

hyperdermic needle

It's an invention that followed from a common accident. Engineers working with injection diesel engines often blasted high-pressure diesel fuel into their bodies. It didn't take long to turn the accident into a new way of delivering medicines. The first jet injector was tried out in 1947.

Jet injectors got a sci-fi boost in 1966 when the TV series *Star Trek* started to show them being used in the future.

A FIXED SMILE

Pierre Fauchard's metal band

We think of braces as a modern thing, but French dentist Pierre Fauchard described using a band of metal to enlarge the mouth in 1728. He wasn't the first. Ancient Greek bodies from 2,400 years ago sometimes have metal bands and animal gut holding teeth together.

The basic design of modern braces was introduced in 1819. Maynard Tucker introduced gum elastics in 1843, and made elastic bands from slices of rubber tubing in 1850.

Some of the first people to benefit from orthodontics, though, were probably already dead. The Etruscans, who lived in Italy 2,500 years ago, used gold wire to bind the teeth of dead bodies so that they would not fall out.

HAIR WHERE THERE WAS NONE

The wig was invented thousands of years ago, in Ancient Egypt or Assyria.

In Ancient Egypt, men and women shaved their heads or cut their hair very short and then wore a wig to protect their head from the harsh desert sun. You might wonder why they didn't just leave their hair in place—but it was a health move to avoid lice.

Wigs were fixed on with beeswax or resin from trees. The wigs could be made of human hair, sheep's wool, or even strands of material from plants. The richest and most important people wore the most ornate wigs.

A QUICK JAB IN AN EMERGENCY

An "epi-pen" is an auto-injector used to give someone a quick, fixed dose of a medicine called epinephrine to prevent a severe allergic reaction.

for bee sting allergy

It is carried by people who know they have dangerous allergies. They can give the injection themselves or someone else can do it for them. The epi-pen is a spring-loaded syringe. The needle shoots out of the end and into the person's thigh when it is used.

The modern epi-pen was developed in the mid-1970s and approved for use in 1987. Auto-injectors were first developed to be used by soldiers to give an antidote to nerve gas used in wars.

for peanut allergy

HAVE FUN, save a BABY

One of the first incubators to save the lives of babies born prematurely (too early) was designed by a French doctor, Stéphane Tarnier. He had seen the chicken incubators at the Paris zoo and thought something similar would help to keep tiny babies warm. He persuaded the director of the zoo to make an incubator for babies.

early incubator

modern incubator

Martin Couney used incubators as a sideshow at fairs from 1893 onward. Visitors paid 25 cents to see a tiny baby inside fighting for its life. It sounds weird, but he made enough money to buy incubators and pay skilled, trained staff to look after the babies at a time when doctors did little for them.

136

YOU CAN SEE HOW YOU'RE DOING ...

Wearable activity trackers monitor what you're doing with your body and what your body's doing itself. They can count the steps you take and some measure your heart rate, and track your sleep.

The first tracker was released in **1982**. The Polar Sports Tester PE2000 needed a chest strap to monitor heart rate, which it displayed on a wrist watch.

Motion sensing in three dimensions was first added to a fitness device in **2006**, giving a better indication of distance covered and calories burned. The first Fitbit was released in **2009**; it clipped onto clothes.

HOLD STEADY!

Broken bones are held still in a cast that allows the patient to move around.

Long ago, people fastened broken limbs to splints of wood, bamboo, or bark using bandages stiffened with all kinds of substances, including wax, ground up shells, egg white, and starch. Patients with a broken leg had to lie in bed while they recovered.

The first plaster casts were developed in the 1850s. Plaster of paris goes rigid after being mixed with water and then dried, so holds a limb steady. A Dutch doctor, Antonius Mathijsen, used plaster of paris bandages with his patients from 1851, while Russian army doctor Nikolai Pirogov developed them separately during the Crimean War of 1853–1856.

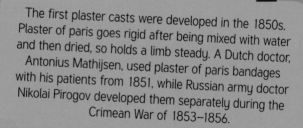

FILLING IN **HOLES**

People have had problems with their teeth for thousands of years. The first filling in a tooth dates from 6,500 years ago and was made of beeswax. It had been fitted carefully to fill a hole.

Fillings made of a mix of mercury and other metals, called "amalgam," were invented in China. They are mentioned in a dentistry text written in 659 BCE. They were introduced to Germany in 1528, and are still used today in a slightly different form.

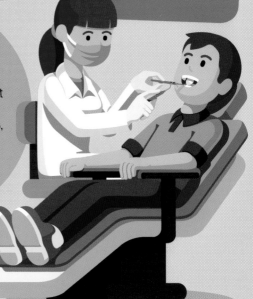

metal filling

CLEAN YOUR TEETH!

The toothbrush was invented in China around **1500**. It had a bone or bamboo handle and bristles from a wild pig.

The first mass-produced toothbrush appeared in England around **1780**.

Toothpaste was invented around **7,000 YEARS AGO** in Ancient Egypt. Egyptians frayed the end of a stick to apply their toothpaste.

Modern toothpaste first came in a jar in the **1850S**.

A toothbrush with nylon bristles was introduced in **1938**.

TOOTHPASTE

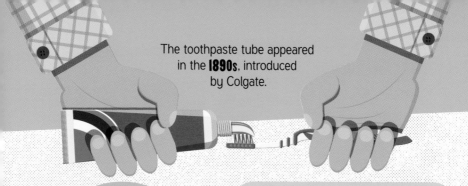

The toothpaste tube appeared in the **1890s**, introduced by Colgate.

A book on dental health published in **1819** suggested people used waxed silk to clean between their teeth— the first dental floss.

Dental floss in a packet with a cutter was introduced in **1882** in the USA.

Ancient Romans used urine as a mouthwash, but the first modern mouthwash was Listerine, invented in **1879**.

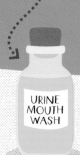

URINE MOUTH WASH

An electric toothbrush invented by Philippe Woog in Switzerland in **1954** had to be plugged into mains electricity while it was used.

141

A HOLE IN YOUR TEETH?
MAKE IT BIGGER!

Dentists don't just stick a filling in a hole in a tooth. First they remove the decayed bits so there's only healthy tooth left. Modern dentists use a high-speed electric drill to do that.

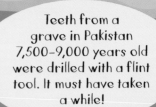

Teeth from a grave in Pakistan 7,500–9,000 years old were drilled with a flint tool. It must have taken a while!

The first mechanical drill for teeth was made by John Greenwood in 1790. It was powered by a treadle operated by the dentist's foot. Greenwood adapted the treadle system from a spinning wheel belonging to his mother. A very noisy clockwork drill followed in 1864, and the first electric drill in 1875.

Cleaning the blood

The kidneys clean toxins (poisons) from the blood. If someone's kidneys don't work, they will die.

Since 1943, though, kidney patients have been able to use **DIALYSIS**—a process that cleans the blood with a machine that works as a fake kidney.

Dutch physician Willem Kolff made the first kidney dialysis machine from sausage skins, orange juice cans, and a washing machine! During World War II, he made five machines, which he later sent to hospitals around the world.

With the war over, nice sparkly new machines could be made with no old washing machines needed.

Willem Kolff ┄┄┄┄>

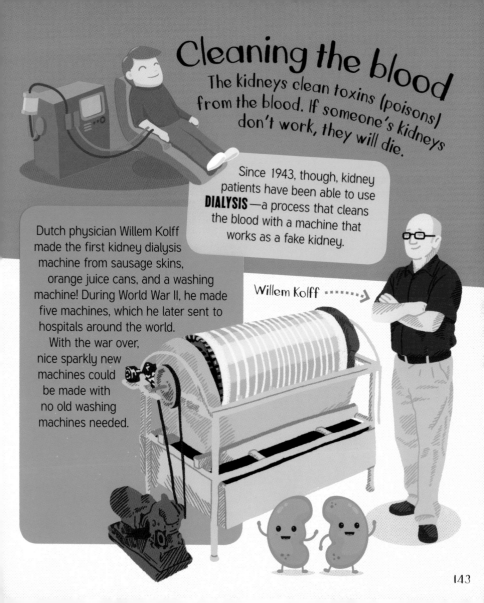

143

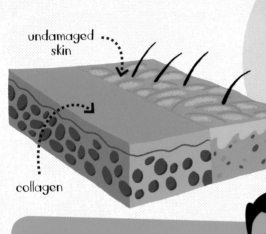

undamaged skin

collagen

NEW SKIN FOR OLD

In 1981, medical scientists were trying to make an artificial skin covering for burns. They failed. But they accidentally invented something even better. They found that if they used thin strands of a natural material called collagen, the body would use it as a framework to regrow the deep layers of skin.

Called Integra™, it's used now to treat people who have serious burns.

These deep layers cannot normally be regrown, and only thick scar tissue appears. The new skin grown over the collagen framework is soft and bendy, much more like normal skin.

144

Reconstructive surgery is used to rebuild parts of a person that have been damaged.

It began in India about 2,700 years ago. Cutting off a criminal's nose was a common punishment, so there was demand for nose surgery.

Surgeons would cut a leaf-shaped flap of skin from the patient's forehead and fold it down over the place the nose should be. They used two hollow stems of a castor oil plant as nostrils and to give the nose shape.

Today, there are many types of reconstructive surgery— but a flap from the patient's forehead is still taken to rebuild a nose.

LEARN TO SAVE A LIFE

If you do a first aid course, you will learn how to help restart someone's breathing or heartbeat with a dummy called a "Resusci Anne," or "Rescue Annie."

It was created in 1958 by Peter Safar and Asmund Laerdal and has a plastic body with "lungs" so that people can learn resuscitation skills.

The face of the dummy is copied from a young woman who drowned in Paris in the 1860s. The man in charge of the morgue where dead bodies were taken took an impression of her face and made plaster copies of it. Safar and Laerdal decided to use the face, known as "L'Inconnue" (the unknown one), for their dummy.

SURGERY BY ROBOT

Surgeons have a lot of skills, but they get tired, their hands shake—and there isn't always one where you need them! Surgical robots have a steady "hand," never tire, and can be sent with people exploring dangerous places, such as space or Antarctica.

Robot surgeons are actually still controlled by a real surgeon—they don't work on their own.

The original surgical robot, called DaVinci, was first used in 2000. It has sensors that act as "eyes" and can handle very fine tools to do detailed work. It can also be controlled at a distance, so a surgeon can use it to help someone far away.

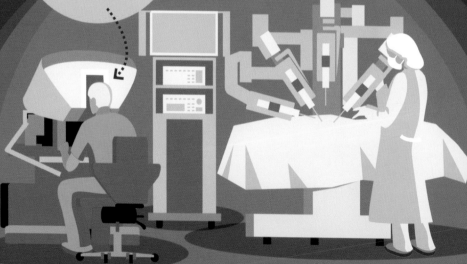

LOOK AFTER YOUR BODY

The first gyms were built **3,000 YEARS AGO** in ancient Persia (now Iran).

Modern-style indoor gymnasiums were invented in Germany. The first opened in Hesse in **1852**.

The first trainers, made in the **1800s**, were heavy and made of leather. Both trainers in a pair were identical—there was no left and right!

Eugen Sandow invented bodybuilding in Germany around **1880**.

The rubber ball was invented in South America around **2,600 YEARS AGO**.

Hand-sanitizer gel was invented in **1966** by nurse Lupe Hernandez.

Canadian James Naismith invented basketball in **1891**.

Liquid shampoo is recent—it was invented in Germany in **1927**.

Soap is much older. A recipe on a Babylonian clay tablet was written down **4,200 YEARS AGO**.

SWAP AROUND!

A transplant moves one or more body parts from one person into another. It can be a life-saving operation.

the Herrick twins

The first successful transplant was a skin graft—moving skin—in **1869**. Then in **1905** Czech surgeon Eduard Zirm transplanted the cornea (transparent outer layer) of an eye.

The first organ transplant was a kidney, moved between two living identical twins Ronald and Richard Herrick in **1954**.

The first operation to use an organ from a dead donor was in **1962**.

A big breakthrough came in **1967** with the first heart transplant, carried out in South Africa by Christiaan Barnard. Now many more body parts can be transplanted, including a hand and even a face.

The tiny stitches needed to stitch blood vessels back together were first developed by the French surgeon Alexis Carrell in France between 1901 and 1910. He took lessons from an expert at embroidery.

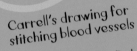

blood vessel

TINY STITCHES

Carrell's drawing for stitching blood vessels

Carrell was inspired to find a way to fix blood vessels after the president of France, Nicolas Léonard Sadi Carnot, was stabbed in 1894. He bled to death because surgeons could not repair a cut blood vessel.

Carrell developed all the techniques of stitching blood vessels still used today. Once surgeons knew how to stitch and repair blood vessels, delicate operations such as transplants became possible.

KICKSTARTING THE HEART

A defibrillator uses a measured electric shock to kickstart the heart into working properly when it is beating irregularly.

The idea was first demonstrated on dogs in 1899. The first defibrillator to use with humans was invented in 1933 by Albert Hyman, an American heart specialist.

Early defibrillators had to be in direct contact with the heart, and so could be used only during an operation on the heart.

The first defibrillator that could be used on the outside of the chest was invented in the USSR, in an area that is now Kyrgyzstan, in the mid-1950s by two doctors, V. Eskin and A. Klimov.

METAL BONES?

Lots of older people have operations to replace worn-out joints, especially hips. The first modern artificial hip joint made of metal was invented in 1940 by American doctor Austin Moore. The rounded "ball" at the top end of the leg bone is removed and replaced by a nice, smooth metal ball that doesn't rub and grate painfully inside the person's hip joint.

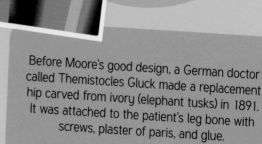

Before Moore's good design, a German doctor called Themistocles Gluck made a replacement hip carved from ivory (elephant tusks) in 1891. It was attached to the patient's leg bone with screws, plaster of paris, and glue.

Long, long ago, people wandered around killing animals for food and picking fruit, roots, berries, seeds, and leaves to eat. It was called being a "hunter-gatherer," and it was a much less reliable way of getting food than going to a store or even farming.

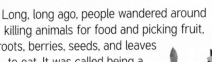

FIRST FARMERS

So eventually people started farming. They would keep animals that they could easily find when it was time to kill and eat them, and they planted edible crops.

Farming was properly invented about 12,000 years ago in the Middle East (around the lands that are now Iraq, Iran, the Levant, and Turkey). People in Israel tried out a little bit of farming as far back as 23,000 years ago, though.

Humans probably chewed sugar cane as soon as they moved into India 60,000 years ago—but that's not quite the same as eating sugar.

SWEET SNACK

The cane dries out quickly, so has to be eaten fresh. To keep sugar for later is tricky. Around 350 BCE, Indian traders wanted to sell sugar to merchants going to and from China.

They found that if they crushed sugar cane so that the sweet juice came out, then left the juice in the sun, the water evaporated, leaving sweet-tasting crystals. And they could take those to markets in Afghanistan and Kazakhstan. They had invented sugar crystals!

155

SWEET, BUT STOLEN

Sugar is not the only sweet food. People have been eating honey for tens of thousands of years.

Other apes eat honey from beehives, and we carried on doing it after evolving into humans. But climbing a tree to raid a hive full of angry bees is a bit risky.

Around 4,400 years ago, people in Ancient Egypt made clay beehives so they had the bees nearby—and low down—and could easily collect their honey whenever they wanted to. There were soon giant honey farms owned by the government with hundreds of hives, and staffed by slaves.

TEA in a BAG

The tea bag was invented accidentally by an American tea merchant, John Sullivan, in the early 1900s.

He provided small samples of his teas in little hand-sewn silk bags. But instead of tipping the tea out as he intended, people put the whole bag into hot water.

The first tea bag packing machine was invented in Germany in 1929.

Only low-grade dust from tea leaves is usually used in tea bags—there's no point wasting good-quality tea on tea bags, as the tea doesn't brew as well in a bag as when it is loose. The dust makes tea more quickly than pieces of leaf, too, as it has a larger surface area.

SMASHED NUTS

Peanut butter became popular in North America after 1884 when Canadian inventor Marcellus Gilmore Edson patented his method of roasting peanuts on a hot surface and grinding them to a paste. He added sugar to make the paste a bit thicker.

Edson wasn't quite first. The Aztecs made a form of peanut butter in Mexico in the 1400s.

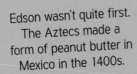

Peanut butter was expensive at first and served at costly health clinics. It was made by Kelloggs (of cornflakes fame) as a food for sick people who needed something that was easy to eat, yet provided a lot of energy.

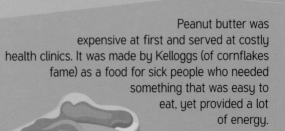

PRAYING FOR PRETZELS

Pretzels were originally soft. Hard pretzels appeared only after they had been introduced to the USA. The first hard pretzel bakery opened in 1850.

According to tradition, pretzels were invented in 610 CE in Italy. A monk wanted to encourage children to learn their prayers, so he devised a treat he could give them when they did so. He made it from strips of bread dough that he folded into a shape like the folded arms of children saying their prayers. He originally called them *pretiola*, which means "little reward," but we know them as pretzels.

FORKS ARE FOR WIMPS

The fork is a newcomer to the silverware drawer. People have used knives and scoops or spoons since the Stone Age, but forks were originally used only during cooking and serving food.

Forks had a hard time when they first came to Europe as tableware. A princess who ate with a fork at her marriage feast in Italy in 1004 CE was mocked for being too fussy. But she was also called ungodly—her critics said "God has given us fingers, so to use a fork is to scorn God!"

Forks spread from Italy to France in 1553 and from there to England and eventually America. Sailors shunned the fork right up until the late 1800s.

WHO NEEDS A FORK WHEN YOU HAVE FINGERS?!

Stick in a CHOPSTICK

While the west was failing to invent forks, the Chinese were successfully inventing the chopstick.

Again, they were first used for cooking and serving food before shrinking and becoming an eating implement. Wooden or bamboo chopsticks were probably invented around 3,600–4,100 years ago, and ivory chopsticks 2,100 years ago.

Silver chopsticks were popular with people who worried they might be poisoned, as they were said to magically reveal poisons in food. In fact, they probably did reveal some poisons used at the time—not magically, but by turning black as the silver reacted with the poison.

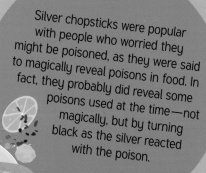

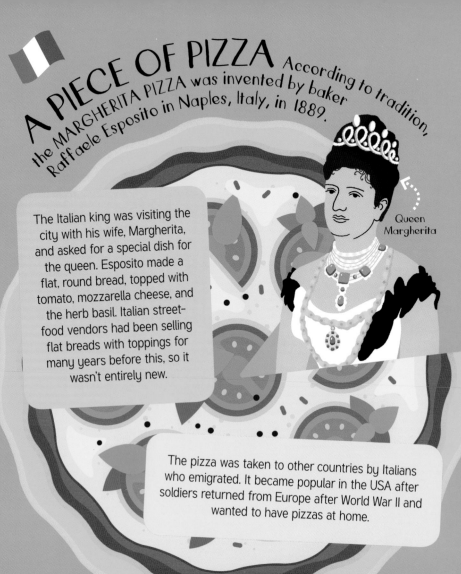

A PIECE OF PIZZA

According to tradition, the MARGHERITA PIZZA was invented by baker Raffaele Esposito in Naples, Italy, in 1889.

Queen Margherita

The Italian king was visiting the city with his wife, Margherita, and asked for a special dish for the queen. Esposito made a flat, round bread, topped with tomato, mozzarella cheese, and the herb basil. Italian street-food vendors had been selling flat breads with toppings for many years before this, so it wasn't entirely new.

The pizza was taken to other countries by Italians who emigrated. It became popular in the USA after soldiers returned from Europe after World War II and wanted to have pizzas at home.

People used actual straws (dried plant stalks) to drink for thousands of years. But straws go soggy.

SUCK IT UP!

Artificial straws made from gold and the precious blue stone lapis lazuli were invented 5,000 years ago in Sumer, in the Middle East. And in Argentina, people used wooden straws for thousands of years.

Drinking through real straws became trendy in Europe and America in the 1800s, but again, people found the straws became soggy. So in 1888, the American inventor Marvin C. Stone invented the paper straw. He wrapped paper around a pencil to make a tube and fixed it with glue.

Marvin C. Stone

Bendy straws were invented in 1937.

SOWING SEEDS SLOWLY— AND SPEEDILY

Until 1701, seed for crops was sown by hand. This meant either scattering the seeds on the ground, or making individual holes for each large seed, such as peas and beans. It was pretty slow, and scattered seed was quickly snaffled up from the surface of the soil by hungry birds.

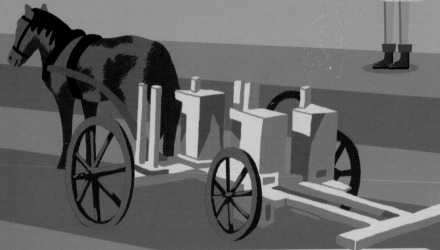

Then, in 1701, the English farmer and inventor Jethro Tull invented a "seed drill." It was a simple machine that could be pushed by hand or pulled by an ox or horse, to cut a furrow in the soil, drop in seeds, and then cover them. It was quicker and much more effective. Crops flourished and farming was revolutionized.

SAY CHEESE!

Cheese was probably invented by accident at least 7,200 years ago.

People used the stomachs of animals killed for meat as containers to transport foodstuffs. When they put milk into a bag made of a stomach, a chemical called **RENNET** in the stomach would have turned the milk to cheese.

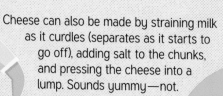

Cheese can also be made by straining milk as it curdles (separates as it starts to go off), adding salt to the chunks, and pressing the cheese into a lump. Sounds yummy—not.

Pottery with tiny traces of cheese on was found in Croatia. It is 7,200 years old.

modern cheesemaking

FAST FOODS

Clarence Birdseye invented the fish finger in **1955**.

Milton Snavely Hershey invented the Hershey bar in **1900**.

... and Hershey's Kisses in **1907**.

Colonel Harland Sanders started selling fried chicken from a roadside restaurant in Kentucky during the Great Depression in **1924**.

The instant dessert Angel Delight was invented in **1967**. It's made by mixing a powder with milk.

The first burger chain in the USA was The White Castle System of Eating Houses, in **1921**.

The first cold breakfast cereal was Graunula, invented by James Jackson in **1863**. It didn't do well, as it had to be soaked overnight.

Pop tarts were invented in **1964**, without sugar frosting. There were four versions—strawberry, blueberry, brown sugar cinnamon, and apple currant.

Frosted pop tarts came along in **1967**.

The first account of jelly beans is a sweet-maker encouraging people to send them to soldiers in the American Civil War, **1861—1865**.

Bagels probably appeared in Poland in the **1300s** when German workers started to make their pretzels in a simpler shape—just a circle with a hole in the middle, called *obwarzanek*.

LOVE it or HATE it ...

YUM!

YUCK!

Marmite is a thick, very dark spread made from brewers' yeast and used on bread or toast in the UK. It's horrible. Or it's lovely. People either love it or hate it.

Marmite was invented accidentally by the German chemist Justus von Liebig in the late 1800s. He found that the sludgy, leftover yeast from brewing beer could be boiled, bottled, and eaten. It's not at all clear exactly why he tried to do that ...

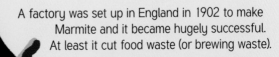

A factory was set up in England in 1902 to make Marmite and it became hugely successful. At least it cut food waste (or brewing waste).

Pancakes were invented in Ancient Greece around 2,500 years ago. It's possible that people came up with pancakes before that, but we don't know about them.

PANCAKES
WITH HONEY?

Early Greek pancakes were made with wheat flour, olive oil, curdled milk, and honey and they were eaten for breakfast. A few centuries later, the Romans added eggs to the pancake batter, making something more like the pancakes we know now.

Pancakes are traditionally eaten on Shrove Tuesday in Europe. It's the start of Lent, a time when people were not supposed to eat anything rich or tasty, so they had to use up all their supplies. They did that by making pancakes.

ORANGES from the SEA?

Tradition tells that marmalade was invented in 1700 in Scotland as a way of using up a shipment of oranges. When a ship full of Seville oranges was damaged in a storm off the Scottish coast, it pulled into Dundee to seek refuge. A local merchant called James Keiller bought all the fruit cheaply. His wife Janet then experimented with it and turned it into a preserve—the first marmalade.

It's probably not true. The technique of shredding oranges supposedly developed by Janet was already being used in England, where people had been eating apple jelly with shredded orange peel in since the 1660s.

IT'S FREEZING!

Quick-freezing is the process used to make frozen food. It was developed by Clarence Birdseye in 1924. You now find Birdseye's name on lots of packets of frozen food.

Birdseye was working in Labrador, Canada, as a fur trader. He noticed that fish he or the Inuit fishermen pulled from the water froze almost immediately in the cold air, but tasted just as good when cooked later. This led him to experiment with rapid freezing methods.

Slow freezing isn't as good—large ice crystals develop in food and break up its structure. When the food is defrosted, some of its taste is lost as the water runs out.

171

FIZZING AND POPPING

Popping candy is a fizzy sweet that "pops" explosively in the mouth. It was invented accidentally by an American chemist, William A. Mitchell, in 1956.

Mitchell was trying to make an instant carbonated soda drink—a powder that could be mixed with water to make something fizzy like cola. It didn't work, so he put his recipe away and forgot about it.

Twenty years later, in 1975, another chemist found his recipe and adapted it to make candy called "Pop Rocks." Instead of dissolving it in water in a glass, he used the fizz of it dissolving in the mouth as its selling point.

COFFEE KEEPS GOATS AWAKE AND IT CAN KEEP YOU AWAKE

Legend tells that coffee was discovered in Ethiopia in the 800s when a goatherd called Kaldi noticed how excitable and lively his goats became after eating the berries of the coffee bush.

Whether or not the story about the lively goats is true, coffee was drunk from the mid-1400s in Arabia. That's where people are first known to have roasted the beans, ground them, and steeped them in water to make a drink. The Sufi used the brew to keep them awake for their religious rituals.

The **HOLE** in a **DOUGHNUT** was invented after the **DOUGHNUT**

The Dutch starting making "olykoeks" in the first half of the 1800s. They were lumps of cake dough fried in animal fat, which doesn't sound quite as yummy as "doughnut."

olykoeks

Hansen Gregory

The middle of the lump of dough didn't cook well as it was too far from the edges. One popular solution was just to stuff the middle with fillings that didn't need to cook (like fruit syrup in a modern doughnut).

But Hansen Gregory, an American ship's captain solved the problem in a different way in 1847—by punching a hole through the doughnut so that there was no undercooked middle.

POPCORN:
DECORATIVE AND DELICIOUS

Popcorn was invented at least 5,600 years ago. Popped kernels have been found in a cave in New Mexico, revealing that cave people made popcorn in their fires.

Popcorn was not only eaten in South and Central American but used to decorate clothes and ceremonial objects.

Colonists moving to the Americas adopted local methods of making popcorn, and some even used it as a breakfast cereal.

Charles Cretors made the first commercial popcorn machine in 1885. He rolled his machine through the streets on a barrow, and popcorn became a popular street snack. Popcorn barrows often served people lining up outside cinemas, forging the link between movies and popcorn.

POPCORN

THE CRETORS

TOAST NEEDS A TOASTER

Alan McMasters made the first electric toaster in Edinburgh, Scotland, in 1893. Before that, people made toast by putting bread in a special frame or impaling it on a toasting fork and holding it in front of a fire or grill.

The first toasters didn't pop up the toast; they just replaced the fire with an electrically heated element. The toast-cook still had to watch it carefully and turn the toast.

A toaster that could flip the toast to cook both sides was invented in 1913, and in 1925 the first modern-style toaster appeared—it could cook both sides at once, pop up the cooked toast, and had a timer.

CHOCOLATE AND MILK GET TOGETHER

cocoa beans

The beans of the cocoa plant have been used for thousands of years, but originally only in drinks. Then in 1847 when Joseph Fry invented a way of making solid chocolate that could be shaped into bars. He added melted cocoa butter (previously removed from the cocoa) back in to make a paste of cocoa, sugar, and cocoa butter. Another British manufacturer, John Cadbury, began making chocolate in 1849.

In 1875, Swiss chocolate-maker Daniel Peter added milk powder to the mix making the first milk chocolate.

177

The first KETCHUP had no tomatoes in it

Ketchup was originally brought to England from the Far East by sailors. In the East, it was a pickled fish sauce added while a meal was cooking—so nothing like modern fish-free ketchup that is added on the plate.

Attempts to recreate the sauce in Europe saw all sorts of ingredients going in, including mushrooms, walnuts, and oysters.

Settlers took ketchup to America, where more things were tried, including tomatoes in 1801. The tomatoes were squeezed, cooked, salted, and bottled with lots of spices. Jonas Yerkes first sold it commercially in 1837. By the end of the century, "tomato ketchup" had become just "ketchup," replacing other varieties.

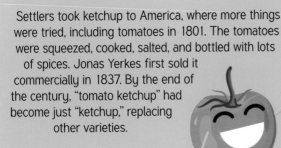

FAST BURGERS

The first quick-cooking burgers were SQUARE! They were developed by Walter Anderson who started The White Castle System of Eating Houses.

Walter Anderson

5¢ HAMBURGER 5¢

5¢ HAMBURGER

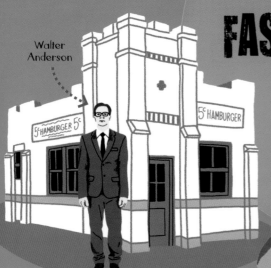

In the 1940s, an employee noticed that if the square burgers, which were called "sliders," had holes in, they cooked more quickly. In 1951 the company patented a square burger with five holes poked in it—the optimum number of holes for cooking quickly and not needing to be turned over.

Having holes also meant the burgers could be cooked over onions and the oniony-taste would go up through the holes and suffuse the burgers.

179

SOGGY WHEAT—
just what you need

When Henry Perky saw someone mushing up wheat with cream to make something easy on the stomach in 1890, he came up with the idea for shredded wheat. He developed a method of processing wheat to make it into long strips that he piled up into biscuits like airy wheat cushions.

Shredded wheat was first sold into vegetarian restaurants in 1892. A vegetarian magazine recommended using shredded wheat as croutons in soup. Original shredded wheat still consists entirely of wheat.

Kyoto

Fortune cookies might seem like they should be a really old tradition—and Chinese. But they started in Kyoto, Japan, in the late 1800s. The cookies were folded around the fortune, but it wasn't inside.

GOOD OR BAD FORTUNE?

The first person to sell the modern-style fortune cookie with the fortune baked inside the cookie was Makoto Hagiwara at a tea garden in California in the late 1890s or early 1900s.

Fortune cookies became associated with China rather than Japan around World War II when Japan was an enemy of the USA.

Attempts to introduce fortune cookies into China in 1992 failed because they were seen as "too American!"

181

You can tell IT'S NOT BUTTER ...

Margarine was invented in 1869 in France by Hippolyte Mège-Mouriès. At the time, France was at war with Prussia (which is now various different European countries) and there was a shortage of butter. The French government offered a prize for anyone who could come up with a substitute for butter that wasn't too horrible and could be produced with ingredients available during the war.

Mège-Mouriès reckoned that cows must make the fat in butter from fat in their own bodies and so he should be able to make something similar if he started with cow-fat. Strangely, it worked.

MILKSHAKES
AREN'T WHAT THEY USED TO BE

The term "milkshake" was first used in 1885 for an alcoholic drink with whisky in.

WHISKY?!!

Milkshakes lost the alcohol and became hand-blended milk drinks made with syrups in the early 1900s.

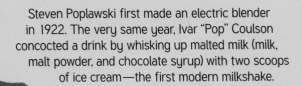

The modern frothy milkshake couldn't be invented until after the electric blender was invented.

Steven Poplawski first made an electric blender in 1922. The very same year, Ivar "Pop" Coulson concocted a drink by whisking up malted milk (milk, malt powder, and chocolate syrup) with two scoops of ice cream—the first modern milkshake.

JUST ADD WATER

Before **1533**, the Incas in Peru ground up and dried potatoes to store them, then mixed the powder with hot water to get mash.

Modern instant mashed potato was invented in Idaho, USA, in **1952** and went on sale as granules in **1955**.

Bisto gravy powder was invented in England in **1908**.

Bisto gravy granules were developed much later than the powder, in **1979**.

TV dinners started with Vesta curries, invented in **1961**. They came dehydrated in a pack and had to be mixed with water to make curry.

Blocks of instant noodles were invented in Japan and went on sale in **1958**.

Cup noodles were introduced in **1971**.

Alphonse Allais invented instant coffee in France in **1881**.

Hot chocolate powder was invented in Holland in **1828**.

In the **1200s**, Mongolian people dried milk to a paste to keep it longer and carry it more easily on horseback.

The first industrial process for making dried milk powder was invented in Russia in **1802**.

SPAM is not just junk mail

Spam is a processed pork product sold in tins. It was invented in 1937 by American Jay Catherwood Hormel who was trying to find a way of selling an under-used part of hogs (pigs), the shoulder. He came up with a method that minced up the meat and stuck it back together with some salt, water, sugar, and starch and then put it in a can so that it could be kept a long time without going off.

SPAM
A NEW HORMEL MEAT

It didn't do well at first as there were other ham products, so Hormel held a competition to give it a snappy name. The winning name, Spam, did the trick. During World War II, 15 million cans a week were fed to allied troops.

THE BEST THING SINCE SLICED BREAD?

Otto Rohwedder's bread slicing machine

People have eaten some form of simple bread for thousands of years, but sliced bread was first sold in the USA in 1928. It was invented by Otto Rohwedder from Iowa, but it took him a long time to get it from a nice idea to a finished loaf. In 1917, his plans and his prototype (early working model) were destroyed in a fire and he had to start again.

Rohwedder did a lot of research into exactly how thick the slices of bread should be, and settled on 1.2 cm (just under half an inch).

187

POP IT IN THE MICROWAVE ...

The microwave oven was designed by American engineer Percy Spencer.

One day, he was experimenting with the magnetrons he worked with; they are vacuum tubes that produce microwave radiation and are used in radar systems. As he worked, he discovered that the chocolate bar in his pocket had melted.

He tried out other foods—an egg shook and then exploded as it expanded inside its shell. Corn popped into popcorn. He realized the microwaves were heating the corn.

In 1945 he registered the design for a microwave oven and in 1947 the first was installed in a restaurant kitchen in Boston.

←······ modern microwave oven

The first microwave ovens for use in ordinary homes came along in 1972.

CUSTARD WITH BIRDS

Alfred Bird

Custard powder was invented by the English chemist Alfred Bird in 1837.

Custard is made from eggs, milk, and sugar, but Bird's wife was allergic to eggs. He devised the powder, which uses cornflour as a thickener in place of eggs, so that she could enjoy custard with her desserts.

BAKING POWDER

Six years later, he was back in the lab inventing baking powder. His wife was also allergic to yeast, so couldn't eat anything raised by yeast, like most bread. Baking powder makes things spongy and light without using yeast. What a lovely husband!

COMBINED HARVESTING

In old-style farming, farm workers had to cut wheat with a scythe, collect it, then separate the wheat grains from the stalks (threshing), and then separate the grains from the husks they grow in (winnowing). It took a long time and was hard work.

Early combine harvesters were pulled by teams of up to 20 horses or mules. George Stockton Berry made the first steam-powered harvester; it burned wheat stalks to heat the water.

In 1826, Scottish clergyman Patrick Bell invented a reaping machine that used blades to cut wheat. American Hiram Moore built the first combine harvester in 1835, based on Bell's reaper. It harvested, threshed, and winnowed all together.

HAPPY MEALS?

MacDonald's was set up in 1948 as a small chain of burger joints by Dick and Mac McDonald.

Happy Meal box

They had their own recipe for making the burgers. They sold their chain to Ray Kroc in 1961 and he built it into a massive international chain.

The success of MacDonald's is built on key products—the Big Mac introduced in 1968 and the Happy Meal in 1979. But MacDonald's weren't the first to come up with the idea of two burgers and three pieces of bun. A sized-up burger was introduced in Big Boy restaurants in 1936.

In the early 1800s, French sweet-maker Nicolas Appert started heating food and packing it in glass jars, a development for which he was richly rewarded by the French government.

CAN WE PUT FOOD IN A CAN?

early can

Another Frenchman, Philippe de Girard, then invented a metal container that could be sealed with food inside, but it was an English inventor, Bryan Donkin, who actually made canned food. He used Girard's design and persuaded the British navy to buy canned beef for sailors in 1813.

Mmm!

MEAT

MEAT

The food was popular with the sailors and credited with saving lives. Sailors who had been sick could eat nourishing meat even when a ship was far from land and supplies of fresh meat.

CAN WE **GET IT OUT** AGAIN?

At first, cans had to be opened with a hammer and chisel. They were made of thick metal and this was quite a challenge. So thick, in fact, that the can usually weighed more than its contents.

Then in **1858** American Ezra Warner invented the can opener—that made things a lot easier! It wasn't like modern can openers, but like a bent knife that had to be driven into the lid and worked around the edge, which sounds dangerous.

A can opener with a toothed wheel was invented in **1870** in the USA, and a second wheel added in **1925**, making the modern can opener.

READY PACKAGED

BEER

The first canned drink was beer, made in Virginia, USA, in **1935**.

ring pull

In **1959**, American Ermal Fraze invented the first pull tab (ring pull) drinks can.

The first clingy plastic wrap was made in **1949** and first sold for household use in **1953**.

The edible "rice paper" found on the bottom of macaroons and some other confectionery is first mentioned in **1634** in China. It's not made from rice, but from stalks of the "rice-paper plant."

Polystyrene cups were invented in **1957**.

Aluminum foil, often used to wrap food, was invented in **1910**. Before that, only tin foil was available.

The Cornish pasty was invented in England more than 500 years ago. It's first mentioned in **1509** or **1510**. The pastry was an edible wrapper for the filling.

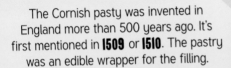

Without the pastry, the pasty is older. Cave paintings **10,000 YEARS OLD** show women eating pasties with leaves as the wrapping.

Buy an ice cream in a cone and you can eat the packaging! It was invented in **1896** by Italian Italo Marchioni in New York.

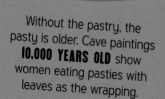

SAUSAGES
are really old

The first mention of a sausage is in a text from Mesopotamia (now part of Iraq) at least 3,000 years old.

Sausages are a natural result of trying to use every bit of a slaughtered animal efficiently. The bits that people maybe don't want to eat as chunks are ground up, mixed together and stuffed into the tubes of the animal's intestines (the original sausage skin), which holds them in shape for cooking.

Sausages seem to have developed independently in lots of parts of the world from the Middle East to China and Europe. Some—"blood sausages"—are just blood and fat in a bit of instestine.

Never too early for ICE CREAM

King Tang

A kind of ice cream was made in China 2,200 years ago when a mixture of milk and rice was frozen using snow. And 1,400 years ago King Tang employed "ice men" who made a dish of frozen buffalo milk, flour, and the oil from camphor trees. The Italian explorer Marco Polo is said to have seen ice cream in China in the 1200s and introduced it to Italy.

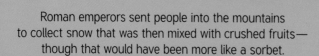

Roman emperors sent people into the mountains to collect snow that was then mixed with crushed fruits—though that would have been more like a sorbet.

SUNDAES ON SUNDAY

The ice cream sundae was invented in America in the late 1800s in the town of Evanston. A law was passed making it illegal to sell ice cream sodas on Sundays in the town for religious reasons.

To get around the ban, people began to make and sell ice cream with syrup replacing the soda. As they had them on Sundays, they called them ice cream sundaes, changing the spelling to make it slightly less obvious that they were flouting the ban on sinfully tasty ice creams treats.

A pressure cooker is a heavy pan that seals completely and cooks food in steam.

UNDER PRESSURE!

As the temperature rises, pressure inside the pan also rises. Cooking food under pressure is quicker than cooking it in an open pan because water can be heated beyond its normal boiling point.

The pressure cooker—or at least the principle of cooking under pressure—was invented by a French physicist in 1679. Denis Papin made a "steam digester" which used the increased boiling point of water under pressure to raise the temperature at which food is cooked. Although it worked, pressure cookers weren't sold for use in cooking until 1864.

Denis Papin's steam digester

SWEET, STICKY— AND, ORIGINALLY, GOOD FOR PEOPLE

Condensed milk is now a sticky, sweet syrup made by evaporating much of the water out of milk and adding sugar. It's used in desserts around the world as it can be stored for years in cans.

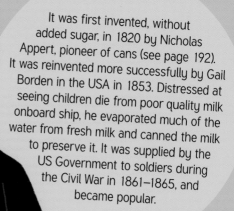

Gail Borden

It was first invented, without added sugar, in 1820 by Nicholas Appert, pioneer of cans (see page 192). It was reinvented more successfully by Gail Borden in the USA in 1853. Distressed at seeing children die from poor quality milk onboard ship, he evaporated much of the water from fresh milk and canned the milk to preserve it. It was supplied by the US Government to soldiers during the Civil War in 1861–1865, and became popular.

A CHILLY ACCIDENT

The popsicle (or ice lolly) was invented accidentally by an 11-year-old kid.

In 1905, Frank Epperson left a mixture of powdered soda and water in a cup on his porch. He had also left a stirring stick in the cup. The temperature dropped overnight and the mixture froze. In the morning, he found the first-ever popsicle on his doorstep.

As an adult, Epperson started selling his ices-on-a-stick under the name **EPSICLE** at a park in California.

His children referred to them as **POP'S SICLES** (from "icicles") and so he changed the name.

NOT WHAT YOU THOUGHT

Ciabatta looks like a traditional Italian bread, and that's what they want you to think. It was invented in **1982** to compete with the baguette (French stick).

ciabatta

baguette

Tea was first drunk in China, perhaps **3,000 YEARS AGO**, as a medicine.

Muesli was invented around **1900** by a Swiss doctor, Maximilian Bircher-Benner, to feed hospital patients.

Quorn mycoprotein, used as a meat replacement, was first produced for sale in **1985**. It's made from a kind of fungus and grown in large vats.

TOMATO SOUP

When Joseph Campbell introduced tomato soup in **1897** tomatoes were never eaten raw as they were thought to be poisonous.

Potatoes have been eaten in South America for thousands of years, but were originally grown for their flowers in Europe. They were first eaten by patients in a hospital in Spain in **1573**.

Cornflakes were not invented to be tasty. John Kellogg introduced them in **1894** as a bland, vegetarian food that would discourage sinfulness.

Fizzy (carbonated) water was the byproduct of a chemical experiment. Joseph Priestley was trying to catch the gas carbon dioxide in **1767** and found it dissolved in water.

French fries were invented in Belgium in the late **1600s** as a replacement for small fried fish when the rivers froze over.

Chocolate was first used in a drink around **4,000 YEARS AGO** in South America. The drink included spices and was not sweet.

The malted milk drink Horlicks was invented in **1897** for sick people—but healthy people liked it, too.

WATERING THE GARDEN COULD BE GROSS ...

To water the garden now, we unreel a plastic hose, all clean and waterproof.

The very first hosepipe was a bit less pleasant. The Greeks made the first fire hoses more than 2,400 years ago—from the intestines of an ox. The intestines were still attached to the stomach at one end, which was filled with water and then squeezed to spray it out onto the fire.

The first artificial hose dates from the 1600s when the Dutch inventor Jan van der Heyden made a hose from leather stitched together. People tried out different materials, including various kinds of oiled cloth and even metal, until rubber took over in 1870.

... OR CIVILIZED

The watering can was invented in 1886 by John Hawes. It replaced the "watering pot" which had been in use since at least 79 BCE, so 2,100 years ago.

Watering pots were metal or stoneware pots with holes in the bottom so that the water fell out like raindrops. There was a hole at the top that was kept covered while moving the pot so that the water couldn't drip out of the bottom too early.

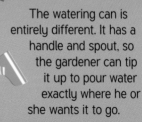

The watering can is entirely different. It has a handle and spout, so the gardener can tip it up to pour water exactly where he or she wants it to go.

ZIP IT!

Zippers are everywhere now, from coats to bags and shoes. Yet the zipper had to be redesigned several times before it really worked.

The first attempt to make an "automatic, continuous clothing closure" was Elias Howe's design in 1851, but he didn't pursue it. The 1890s saw Whitcomb Judson's "clasp locker," intended for shoes, but that also failed. The modern form of the zip fastener was invented in 1913 by Gideon Sundback. The name "zipper" came later, in 1922.

Zip fasteners were first used for boots and tobacco pouches, only making it to clothes after another 20 years had passed. Men's trousers were the first clothing to sport zip fasteners.

Gideon Sundback's zip design

PASS THE TISSUES

A box of thin pieces of fragile paper hardly seems like an invention at all. But it is—the box of tissues didn't exist before 1924.

Kleenex was the first brand of tissues and it's still growing strong. Although we now use tissues mostly for nose-blowing, that's not what they were intended for. Their first use was to help actors remove their stage and screen make-up. Actors would smear cold cream on their face and use a tissue to wipe it off, taking the make-up with it. But the public found a new use for tissues, replacing the handkerchief.

In Japan, people have used small squares of thin pieces of paper as disposable hankies for centuries and have traditionally considered fabric hankies quite disgusting.

207

Before the **TISSUE,** the **HANDKERCHIEF**

It's possible that in Ancient Greece and Rome, people already used the fabric handkerchief. But that age faded away.

Richard II

According to tradition, the modern cloth handkerchief started with the Richard II, who was king of England from 1377 to 1399. His courtiers wrote about him using a square of fabric to wipe his nose, at a time when the "kerchief" was usually used to cover the head. Imagine the strange looks you'd get if you started to wipe your nose on your scarf!

NOT JUST FOR THE NOSE

Some people used tissue paper to wipe other parts of their bodies.

Toilet paper might seem like a modern invention, but, in China, wealthy people were using paper to wipe themselves after going to the toilet 2,200 years ago.

Elsewhere, people used all kinds of things, from fabric to bits of plant or even stones, or just washed with water.

In Ancient Rome, a sponge on a stick was the preferred method of cleaning the bottom. The sponge was washed after use, and often stored in a pot of vinegar.

The first modern commercial toilet paper was invented by Joseph Gayetty in the USA in 1857.

FLUSH
IT AWAY

From holes in the ground to simple plumbing systems there were ways of getting rid of waste long before the invention of the flush toilet. The first simple plumbed toilets might have been invented in India 6,000 years ago, or Scotland 5,000 years ago.

The first semi-modern loo was invented in **1592** by Sir John Harrington, godson of the English Queen Elizabeth I. He made one for himself and one for the Queen and that was it for nearly 200 years.

Then in **1775** the watchmaker Alexander Cummings added an S-shaped bend to a pipe below a toilet to trap smells. Toilets became a bit more popular, but in cities during the 1800s, there might still be just one toilet shared by 100 people.

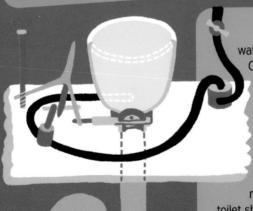

A LIGHT-BULB MOMENT

Everyone thinks Thomas Edison invented the light bulb in 1879. No doubt he would be very pleased about that, but it's not quite that simple.

Thomas Edison

The English chemist Humphrey Davy first discovered that passing an electric current through a thin metal wire makes it glow, but he didn't have a way of making it last long enough to be useful. Another British chemist, Warren de La Rue, solved the problem using platinum in a vacuum. But the cost of the platinum and the difficulty of creating a vacuum in the bulb made his invention uneconomic.

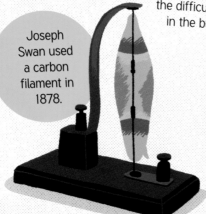

Joseph Swan used a carbon filament in 1878.

Edison's contribution was a better vacuum and a thinner carbon filament, refining something already invented.

STICKY TAPE

wasn't sticky enough

Richard Gurley Drew first invented masking tape in 1925 to help people painting cars to get a clean line between two shades of paint. His first tape fell off as there wasn't enough glue. Frustrated car workers referred to Drew's "Scotch bosses," meaning they were too stingy to use enough glue. He came back with stickier tape, but it's still known as Scotch tape in the USA.

Drew invented the first transparent sticky tape in 1930. Even though it was the Great Depression (a time of widespread poverty) it was successful, as it allowed people to save money by mending things.

A STITCH IN TIME ... CAN BE DEADLY

People have been sewing clothes for 20,000 years, beginning with bone needles and thread made of animal sinew. Today we have clean thread and metal needles—and sewing machines.

A French tailor, Barthélemy Thimonnier, built the first working sewing machine in **1830**. Other tailors were furious as they saw it threaten their business, and burned down his factory while he was in it.

In America, Walter Hunt invented a sewing machine in **1834**. He was conscience-stricken when he thought of the jobs that could be lost, and didn't register his design. Finally, in **1844** the English inventor John Fisher came up with the "lockstitch" design that uses two threads, one above and one below, and is still used now.

213

It's astonishing that no one thought of putting wheels on a suitcase until 1970.

THE INVENTION THAT ALLOWS YOU TO TAKE TOO MUCH LUGGAGE

The idea occurred to Bernard D. Sadow when he was struggling to handle two heavy suitcases after a flight and saw an airport worker move a large piece of equipment on a wheeled trolley.

He made a wheeled suitcase and tried to sell it to some shops, with little success at first. Stores told him men wouldn't buy it as they didn't want to look weak and weedy. But they did, even though his wheeled suitcases had four wheels.

In 1987, Northwest Airlines pilot Robert Plath invented the modern wheeled suitcase with a telescopic handle and two wheels, rolling upright.

A MONOPOLY ON **MONOPOLY**?

The popular board game Monopoly was patented by Charles Darrow in the USA in 1935. The story goes that Darrow invented the game during the Great Depression to remind his family that times had not always been so hard. He sold the game to Parker Brothers and it became a bestseller, making everybody rich.

But that's not the whole story. A game very like Monopoly, called the Landlord's Game, was invented 30 years earlier by Elizabeth Magie. The point of her game was educational— to teach people about the evils of an economic monopoly, when one small group controls most of the wealth and business.

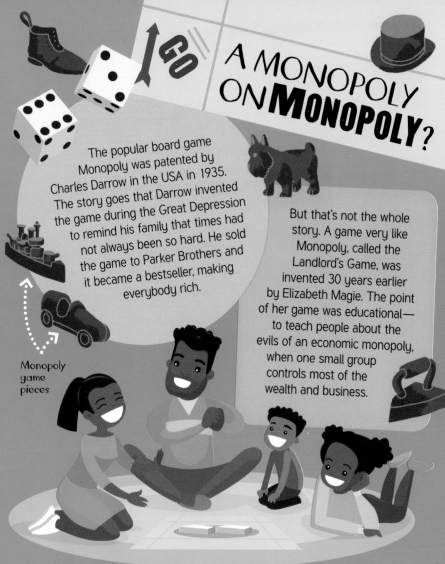

Monopoly game pieces

THE **YO-YO** AS STRESS-BEATER

The yo-yo might have been invented in Ancient China, but was first mentioned 2,500 years ago in Greece.

From 1765, the modern yo-yo spread around Europe, apparently from India. It was popular with the nobility, and was used to de-stress. Some French aristocrats played with their yo-yos on the way to be executed during the French Revolution, and Napoleon's army relaxed with yo-yos on the eve of the Battle of Waterloo in 1815.

Meanwhile, people in the Philippines perfected the wooden yo-yo with a modern design and it was from there that it was introduced to the USA in the 1920s.

POWER FOR THE PEOPLE

The very first battery was made by the Italian scientist Alessandro Volta in 1800. It consisted of a pile of disks made of copper and zinc, separated by circles of cloth or cardboard soaked in salt water. Connecting wires to the metal circles at each end, he could make a full electrical circuit. His battery was called the "voltaic pile."

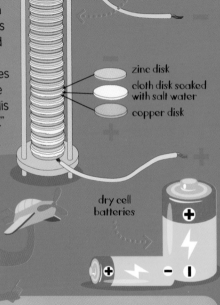

voltaic pile

zinc disk

cloth disk soaked with salt water

copper disk

The current is produced by electrons moving from one substance to another in a chemical reaction. It wasn't the sort of thing you could have put in a torch or cycle light.

dry cell batteries

The first dry cell battery, that couldn't spill its contents, was invented in 1886. Mass-produced batteries went on sale in 1896, making small electric devices possible.

SHINING A LIGHT

The dry-cell battery made possible the invention of the flashlight. Before this, people had to use a lantern or burning torch if they wanted a portable light, and these always carried a risk of fire.

first flashlight

The first flashlight was invented in 1899 by the British inventor David Misell. It consisted of a cardboard tube containing batteries laid end-to-end with a bulb and reflector at one end. Missell gave some flashlights to the New York City police force, which was a shrewd move as it gave him publicity.

The first flashlights were expensive and not very bright, but improved bulbs and batteries in 1904 made them much more useful and popular. Unlike a lantern, they could be turned on instantly.

SNIP-SNIP

→ early
scissors

The first scissors or shears were "spring" scissors used in the Middle East 3,000–4,000 years ago. They had two blades connected by a thin metal band. Squeezing brought the blades together, cutting whatever lay between them. This style of scissors or shears was used around the world for centuries.

Modern scissors with a pivot between the handles and blades became popular after 1761 when Robert Hinchliffe of Sheffield, England, first made them. To start with, he made the handles solid, then filed holes for the user's fingers to go through.

IT'S ALL FUN AND GAMES

The crime-solving board game **CLUE** (or **CLUEDO**) was invented by retired legal clerk Anthony Pratt in 1944.

Nintendo invented the **GAMEBOY** handheld games console in 1989.

MOUSE TRAP—originally called the Mouse Trap Game—was invented in 1963. Players compete to build a working plastic mouse trap and catch each other's mice.

PING-PONG, or table tennis, was invented in the 1880s when tennis players brought their game indoors in bad weather.

The handheld digital "pet" **TAMAGOTCHI** was invented by Akihiro Yokoi and Aki Maita in Japan in 1996.

The quiz game **TRIVIAL PURSUIT** was invented in 1979 by two Canadians, Chris Haney and Scott Abbott.

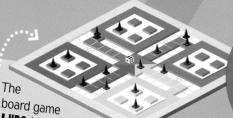

The board game **LUDO** (or **PARCHEESI**) started as Pachisi, played in India 1,500 years ago. It was brought to Europe by the British in the late 1800s.

The word game **SCRABBLE** was invented by American Alfred Mosher Butts in 1938.

Satoshi Tajiri came up with idea for **POKÉMON** in 1989. The first games were released in 1996.

George Hansburg invented the **POGO STICK** in 1919. The first shipment of wooden "jumping sticks" rotted on the sea crossing, so he redesigned it in metal.

The **BARBIE DOLL** was invented by American Ruth Handler in 1959. The first black Barbie was released in 1980.

221

COMPUTER GAMES ARE NEARLY AS OLD AS COMPUTERS

The very first computer game was tic-tac-toe. A computer exhibited at a show in 1950 could play a form of tic-tac-toe, but it was intended only to impress people by showing what the computer could do.

The first game actually made to have fun was "Tennis for Two" in 1958. It was an on-screen tennis game in which players had to knock a "ball" backward and forward on the screen.

The first game not tied to one computer was "Spacewar!" It was invented in 1961 by students at Stanford University, USA, and was soon installed on computers in other universities. Two players each controlled a spaceship and had to battle their opponent, using a specially built control box.

Computer games got out of the universities and onto coin-operated games machines in bars and clubs in the 1970s. The earliest, **COMPUTER SPACE**, was released in 1971. A player had to shoot down flying saucers from their spaceship.

FUN
FOR ALL

The game that really took off and made computer games popular was a simple on-screen ping-pong game called **PONG**, produced by Atari in 1972.

Soon people wanted to play games not just in the arcade but at home. The first games consoles were hardwired to play just one game, but by 1976, the first that could have different games switched in appeared, the **FAIRCHILD CHANNEL F** (F for "fun"). The modern age of computer gaming began.

223

SWAP YOU!

Trading cards are a product on their own now, but they were originally given away.

In **1888**, two tobacco companies started printing cards with advertisements that they put into their packets of cigarettes, and two years later this changed to pictures of other things.

By **1900**, 300 companies were producing collectible sets of pictures on themes including sport, war and nature. Children began asking adults for the cards, collecting and swapping them.

Cigarette cards ended with the paper shortage of World War II. After the war, cards were added to other products—packs of tea in Britain and bubble gum in the USA. Cards were first sold alone, without the gum, in **1981**.

A SPRINGY LAMP

The Anglepoise is a desk lamp that can be angled in any direction and stay there.

It sounds pretty basic, but it was only invented in 1934 after a car designer, George Carwardine, developed a new kind of spring and lever mechanism. Carwardine invented his lever system in 1932—and then looked for a way to use it. He came up with the idea of an adjustable work lamp.

A special design of Anglepoise to use in planes was introduced in 1939. It was made entirely from non-magnetic materials so that it didn't interfere with flight instruments.

GLUE FOR GUNSHOT WOUNDS

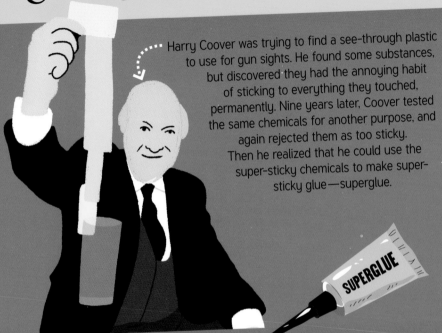

Harry Coover was trying to find a see-through plastic to use for gun sights. He found some substances, but discovered they had the annoying habit of sticking to everything they touched, permanently. Nine years later, Coover tested the same chemicals for another purpose, and again rejected them as too sticky. Then he realized that he could use the super-sticky chemicals to make super-sticky glue—superglue.

SUPERGLUE

During the Vietnam War (1955–1975), medics discovered that if they sprayed superglue into open wounds, the victims stopped bleeding almost immediately. It saved millions of lives. Now, special medical-grade superglue is used to close wounds.

A FIRE EXTINGUISHER powered by, er, FIRE ...

The first known fire extinguisher was invented in 1723 by English chemist Ambrose Godfrey. It consisted of a container of fire-suppressing liquid and a small pewter canister of gunpowder connected to a system of fuses. To use the fire-extinguisher, a person had to set light to a fuse (no problem finding something to light it with!). The gunpowder would make a small explosion, scattering the liquid over the fire.

The first modern style of dry-powder fire extinguisher was invented by English army captain George Manby in 1818. It contained 3 gallons (13.6 l) of "pearl ash" (potassium carbonate) held in compressed air.

ROLLED OVER

When Canadian Norman Breakey invented the paint roller to make decorating a house easier, he hoped to make good money. But he couldn't make his rollers quickly enough to sell many. His roller consisted of a central cylinder covered with fabric that would soak up the paint, then deposit it on a wall when rolled over the surface.

Such a straightforward design is easy to copy, and that's just what happened. Other people made small changes to his design then registered it as their own. Many of them were far more successful financially than Breakey himself, who died in poverty.

PAPER FOR WALLS (AND BALLOONS)

People have been decorating their walls with paper since at least the early **1500s**. At first, instead of a repeated pattern, they had large pictures made up of several sheets of paper pasted to the wall.

Patterned papers became popular in the **1700s**. Most wallpapers were made in England or France.

Some of the finest hand-printed papers were produced by the French manufacturer Jean-Baptiste Réveillon. One of his papers was used on the outside of the Montgolfier's first hot-air balloons in **1783**.

The first machine to print wallpapers in different shades was invented in France in **1785** by Christophe-Philippe Oberkampf.

229

A QUICK BLOW DRY

The hairdryer was first invented for use in hairdressing salons. Alexandre-Ferdinand Godefroy introduced his "hair dressing device" in **1888** in a salon in France. It had a cover for the client's wet head that attached to the chimney pipe of a gas stove. It didn't effectively move the air much and the device was fixed in one place, which was inconvenient.

Gabriel Kazanjian registered the first design for a blow-dryer in **1911**. The first handheld hairdryers went on sale in the USA and became popular in the **1920s**.

WORKING LIKE CLOCKWORK

Clockwork mechanisms have a system of gears, and generally a tightly wound spring that unwinds slowly.

The earliest known clockwork mechanism is the Antikythera mechanism, which was made in Greece more than 2,000 years ago and was found in an ancient shipwreck in 1901. It was used for calculating and predicting the movement of the Sun and Moon across the sky.

Europeans then seem to have forgotten about clockwork for around 1,000 years, until it was reintroduced through the Islamic world. Around 1300, European towns began building clock towers with clockwork clocks. But they had only one hand, telling the hour, so no precisely scheduled events!

231

TIME'S UP!

The sun dial was the first time-telling device, made at least **3,500 YEARS AGO**. The position of a shadow shows the approximate time of day—if it's sunny!

The hourglass was first used around **1,300 YEARS AGO** in Europe.

The first watches were chunky cylinders worn on a neck-chain from the late **1400s**. They had only an hour hand.

The Italian scientist Galileo discovered how pendulums work and designed a clock in **1637**, but didn't build it.

Dutch astronomer Christiaan Huygens added a pendulum to a clock in **1656**. This kept it accurate even as the clock wound down.

The first digital pocket watch used a mechanical display of numbers. It was invented in **1883** by Austrian engineer Josef Pallweber. He called it a "jump-hour" clock.

Jost Burgi added the first minute hand to a clock in **1577**.

The first mechanical alarm clock, invented in **1787**, could only go off at 4 am!

An adjustable alarm clock that could be set for any time was invented in **1876**.

The first battery-powered clock went on sale in **1912**.

Swiss inventor John Harwood made the first self-winding watch in **1923**.

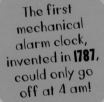

233

BAG IT OR BIN IT

Before garbage bags, people had to clean their smelly garbage cans.

Then in the 1950s, Canadian inventor Frank Plomp started to make polyethylene film garbage bags in his kitchen. He first sold them to hospitals and businesses as a way of saving money on cleaning garbage cans (bins). In 1962, he persuaded the town of Waterloo, near Vancouver, to get residents to use the bags. He made special green bags for household use so that they wouldn't look unsightly while waiting to be picked up.

Now, garbage bags look like a very bad idea. They don't biodegrade and cause damage in the environment.

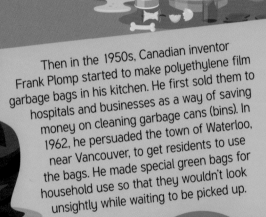

234

Keep your food HOT—or COLD

A vacuum flask is good for taking hot soup on an outdoor trip in winter, or a cold drink to a hot sports day.

It was invented in 1892 by the British scientist James Dewar. He began by putting one bottle inside another and pumping the air out of the gap between them, making a vacuum. That meant heat couldn't travel by convection between the two bottles. Then he added reflective foil to the surface of the inner bottle to reflect radiant heat back into the bottle's contents.

- stopper
- foil surface on inner bottle
- outer bottle
- vacuum
- hot or cold liquid
- metal/plastic container

He should have become rich, but he didn't register his design. Two German glassblowers copied his idea and made their own flasks, forming a company called "Thermos" which made a fortune from the design.

KNIT-WIT

Today, people who knit do it because they like to, but originally knitting was an important way of making clothes.

The first knitting machine, invented in 1589, made the process much quicker.

The English clergyman William Lee made the first machine for knitting stockings and socks. It copied the action of human knitters but used at least 8 needles at a time. It was possibly his worst idea ever.

OFF WITH HIS HEAD!

Queen Elizabeth I refused to let him register his design as it would put knitters out of work. He went into business with a partner anyway, but the partner was executed for treason in 1603. He moved to France, but died in poverty in 1614.

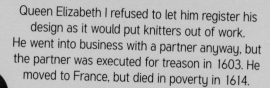

LIQUID SOAP
–and getting it out of the bottle!

SOAP

In **1865**, William Sheppard registered his process for making an "improved" liquid soap, which suggests there was already some kind of liquid soap but it wasn't very good. Other companies soon began making liquid soaps. Most were sold to factories and hospitals.

Liquid soap to use at home didn't appear until **1980**. Minnetonka Corporation of Minnesota released their liquid soap, but were aware other businesses would try to move in on the market. To protect their business, they bought up the entire supply of plastic soap dispenser bottles. No one would buy liquid soap unless they could get it out of the bottle! Until **1987**, Minnetonka had the market pretty well cornered.

WHEN INVENTIONS DO HARM ...

The cotton gin is a mechanical device for separating the fluffy natural threads of cotton from the seeds that grow inside it. The first cotton gins were used in India 1,500 years ago.

When Eli Whitney invented a cotton gin in America in 1793 it made cotton-growing much more profitable. The unintended result was that slavery increased in America. The ability to make money out of cotton led to cotton farmers buying slaves to grow and harvest cotton.

Whitney's machine pulled threads of cotton from a big ball of cotton fluff while seeds fell through a wire mesh into a tray below.

raw cotton

PAC-MAN

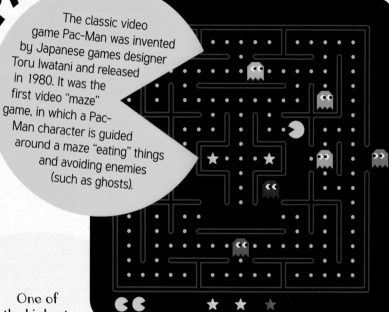

The classic video game Pac-Man was invented by Japanese games designer Toru Iwatani and released in 1980. It was the first video "maze" game, in which a Pac-Man character is guided around a maze "eating" things and avoiding enemies (such as ghosts).

One of the highest-grossing of all video games, it's made about US$12 billion (at 2019 prices). As Iwatani was an employee of game company Namco when he invented the game, he did not make extra money from it.

Pac-Man began on video arcade consoles in bars and clubs, but soon became available on personal computers and handheld game consoles.

FAST FABRICS

People began using a handheld spindle to spin a twisted strand of thread or yarn **7,000 YEARS AGO**.

Spinning meant people could make ropes and fabrics. The Ancient Egyptians couldn't have made mummies without making fabric bandages!

The spinning wheel was used in India **1,000–1,500 YEARS AGO**. It might have been invented there, or possibly started in China even earlier.

foot treadle

The spinning wheel is faster than a handheld spindle. Adding a foot-operated treadle in the early **1500s** made it faster still.

In **1764**, British carpenter James Hargreaves invented the "spinning jenny," which could produce eight threads at a time with a single wheel.

He soon added further spindles, up to 120 threads at a time. Spinning moved from something people did at home to factory work.

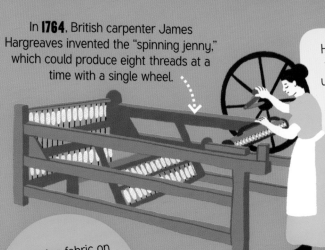

Weaving fabric on a loom began **7,000 YEARS AGO** in the Middle East. The first material used was flax, to make linen.

Weaving moved into factories, becoming an industrialized process from **1785**.

John Kay invented the "flying shuttle" in **1733**, making mechanized weaving faster and easier.

purse from earliest crochet pattern 1823

The Jacquard loom, invented in **1803**, could be programmed with punched cards to weave patterns. It later inspired computer programming.

Knitting and sewing are very old, but crochet (using one hooked needle) was invented in **1823** or soon before.

241

HOW BOUNCY IS A WALRUS?

The first form of trampoline was a walrus-skin blanket held taut by a group of people while another bounced on it! The dancer on the "trampoline" was thrown into the air by those holding the blanket as part of the Inuit spring celebration of the whale harvest, called Nalukataq.

The first modern trampoline was made by George Nissen and Larry Griswold in 1936 in Iowa, USA. Both were gymnasts. They had seen trapeze artists bouncing up from the safety nets under their equipment to make their display more entertaining, and developed a canvas trampoline for bouncing deliberately. It was first intended for training acrobats but soon people began to use it in its own right.

242

George Washington Ferris built the first Ferris wheel for the 1893 Chicago World's Fair. His wheel held 1,400 passengers at a time and was 80.4 m (264 ft) high. Ferris was a bridge-builder, and interested in demonstrating the usefulness and strength of structural steel. From the top of his wheel, passengers could see for 80 km (50 miles); it took 20 minutes to make a full turn.

A FUN TURN

Ferris's wheel was taken down and rebuilt a few times, but was too large to store. In World War I, the metal was used to build a ship, the USS *Illinois*.

Smaller wooden wheels with swinging chairs attached had been used at European fairs since at least the early 1600s.

243

FUN WITH ICE AND STEEL

The modern rollercoaster has its origins in a kind of novelty slide constructed in Russia in the 1600s. The slides were built each winter from ice and a wooden framework. They were 21–24 m (70–80 ft) high and had a thrilling 50 degree drop.

The first modern rollercoaster opened in Paris in 1817. The carts were locked to the track, and guide rails kept them going the right way—safety features that meant they could go fast with not too much risk of disaster. The first gravity switch-back rollercoaster ride was built in Coney Island, USA, by LaMarcus Adna Thompson in 1884.

REBUILDING LIFE AS A SIM

The computer simulation game *The Sims* was the first modern simulation game in which players build entire homes and cities and populate them with simulated people.

American games designer Will Wright came up with the idea for *The Sims* after his real house was destroyed in a wildfire in 1991. Having to rebuild his home and restock it with possessions led him to try to recreate that experience as a computer game. He said he also intended it as a criticism of American consumerism, and that he based the design on theories about the way people think and what they want from life.

PINGING THINGS ACROSS LAND AND SEA

If you've got a rubber band, you can make a catapult. It's used as a toy now, but was originally invented as a weapon.

The Ancient Greek Dionysius the Elder invented the catapult 2,400 years ago. He was looking for a new kind of weapon and came up with a device for throwing large rocks.

coiled rope is released, unwinding quickly to throw the launching arm upward

launching arm

winch to wind rope, storing energy

If you make a catapult with a rubber band, the energy for hurling the object is stored in the stretched rubber band. Ancient Greeks didn't have rubber bands, and instead pulled back the launching arm of the catapult with a rope coiled round a wooden bar.

BRIGHT, BRIGHT SUN

Nearly 2,000 years ago, the Roman emperor Nero used to watch gladiators in the arena using an emerald, either looking through it to cut the bright sun or as a mirror, watching in a reflection. From 900 years ago, people in China looked through panes of smoky quartz to protect their eyes from the sun.

Inuit people have long used goggles with a tiny slit to cut the amount of light reaching their eyes, but these have no lenses.

The French chemist Antoine Lavoisier used tinted glasses when experimenting with focusing sunlight in 1772. Lenses to block damaging ultraviolet rays were invented in 1913, and sunglasses became popular in the 1920s. American Sam Foster introduced the first mass-produced sunglasses in 1929.

247

MONEY, MONEY, MONEY ...

Before there was money, people bartered, swapping things they had for things they needed. Money makes trade easier. For example, you can sell a sheep for money and use the money to buy carrots from someone who didn't want a sheep.

The first money was not coins but other token objects like shells and beads. The first metal coins we know about were made 2,700 years ago in China, India and near Greece.

Paper money first appeared in China about 1,000 years ago. It was issued when there was a shortage of metal for making coins. It caught on as it was easier to carry a few pieces of paper than a lot of heavy metal coins.

The piano is one of the most popular musical instruments in the world, yet it's not very old.

It was invented just before 1700 in Italy by Bartolomeo Cristofori, who was employed to look after an Italian duke's collection of musical instruments. Not content with looking after those he already had, Cristofori invented a new one.

PIANO, PIANO

The first pianos had fewer keys than a modern piano, and had no pedals.

Some other instruments are much older. The trumpet was used by armies 3,500 years ago (though in a simpler form, as a horn). Alligator skin drums have been found in China that are at least 4,500 years old.

DOGS, BURRS, AND VELCRO

The Swiss engineer George de Mestral went walking in the mountains with his dog in 1948. When he got home, he had to remove sticky burrs from his clothes and his dog's coat and decided to look at them under the microscope. On seeing that the burrs were covered with tiny hooks, he set about making a fastener that used the same method.

Eight years later, de Mestral perfected Velcro. It consists of two strips of fabric, one covered with tiny plastic hooks and the other covered with tiny loops.

Velcro became successful and popular after NASA began to use it in the 1960s to secure objects and clothing on spaceflights.

close up of Velcro

SNAP FASTENERS
FOR TERRACOTTA ARMY HORSES

The oldest known snap fasteners (also called poppers or press studs) were made in ancient China more than 2,200 years ago. An army of life-size terracotta warriors and their horses was entombed with the dead emperor Qin Shi Huang. Snap fasteners were used to connect removable halters on the horse figures.

Terracotta Army

SNAP!

The modern snap fastener was invented by German inventor Heribert Bauer in 1885, which was 90 years before the Terracotta Army was discovered buried under a hill. They were intended as an unusual and fun fastener for men's trousers.

SMALL, BUT REALLY USEFUL

Stephen Perry invented the rubber band in **1845** for holding bundles of papers together.

The first wall paint to use straight from the can was invented in **1866** by the American company Sherwin-Williams.

Austrian Franz Greiter produced the first successful modern sun cream in **1938**.

He also introduced the SPF scale for strength of sun cream in **1962**.

SUN CREAM
SPF 30

The drawing pin or thumbtack was invented in America in the **MID–1750S**.

German inventor Friedrich Soennecken registered the first design for a hole-punch in **1886**.

The first type of stapler, invented in **1867**, pushed the staple through paper but didn't bend it closed.

A stapler that also bent the staple to close it came along in **1868**.

In **1858**, Hymen Lipman registered his design for a pencil with an eraser on the end.

The magnifying glass, or a lens to make things look larger, was first described in Ancient Greece nearly **2,500 YEARS AGO**.

Matches that burn when struck were invented in **1805** in France by Jean Chancel.

The lock and key were first invented in the Middle East, as much as **5,000 YEARS AGO**.

253

SOME THINGS ARE TOO SMALL TO SEE

—or were until the microscope was invented in the 1590s.

modern microscope

It's now impossible to imagine not knowing there are things too small to see, from the hairs on a bug to bacteria. The microscope opened up a whole new world, previously unimagined.

The first microscopes used two lenses to focus a magnified image.

No one is quite sure who invented the microscope. Top contenders are Hans and Zacharias Janssen, a father-and-son team of spectacle-makers who lived in Holland, or Hans Lippershey, who lived in the same town.

earliest microscope

The telescope opened up another whole new world— or several, in fact.

AND SOME THINGS ARE TOO FAR AWAY TO SEE

The first telescope was probably made in 1608 in Belgium or Holland, possibly by Hans Lippershey. He first registered a design, but might not have been the first to make a telescope.

Galileo

When the Italian scientist Galileo turned his improved telescope to the night sky, he saw craters on the Moon, that the Milky Way is a band of stars, and that the planets are other worlds—an Earth-shattering discovery.

The telescope helped persuade people that Earth goes around the Sun and not the other way around. And by showing other worlds, it led to the idea of alien life.

YOU MIGHT NOT WANT TO FIX EVERY CREAKY FLOORBOARD...

special clamp

A creaky floor doesn't sound like a clever invention—but in Ancient Japan, a "nightingale floor" was built with loose floorboards to make a noise as an alarm system.

From the 1600s, some wealthy people built homes with wooden floors in which the floorboards weren't nailed down firmly. A special clamp under the loose boards rubbed against a nail if the floorboard moved as someone stepped on it—the someone being a sneaking thief or assassin. They were so cleverly made that walking more softly made a louder noise!

If you visit Kyoto in Japan, you can even try creeping over a nightingale floor.

IT KEEPS YOUR BANANA SAFE

If you've ever found a mushed banana in your lunchbox you know you need the BANANA GUARD.

It's a plastic box, the same shape as a banana. You can put it in your bag and your banana is safe from being crushed, no matter how many other things you want to carry around.

Banana guards are pretty common now, but the when they were first invented in 2003 they looked like a crazy idea. Perhaps because the first design was called the "banana suitcase" and also had a foam lining to keep the banana nicely snuggled. That's pushing banana comfort too far.

TURN YOURSELF INTO A BOAT

It's easiest to catch fish if you go out into the water where the fish are. Usually, that requires a boat, which is extra expense for the fisherman or fisherwoman. But a device invented in 1990 lets you turn yourself into a boat.

The fisherperson sits on a float, dragging another float that holds a large battery. The battery drives a motor that rotates a propeller strapped to the fishperson's leg. They wear a flipper on the opposite foot. Then with the propeller-leg held out straight, they use that to drive forward and the other leg as a rudder to steer.

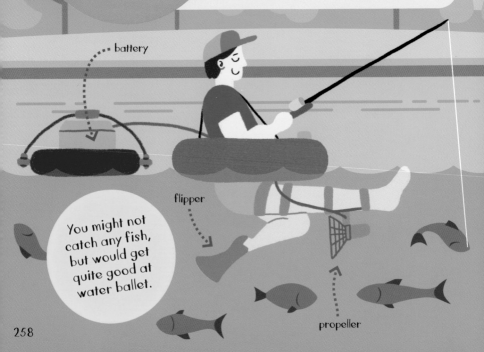

battery

flipper

You might not catch any fish, but would get quite good at water ballet.

propeller

Who needs all that metal frame between the wheels of a bicycle? You can be your own bicycle frame as long as you've got a regular body with two arms and legs.

The "body-connected bike" was invented in 2004. The front wheel has handles on either side for the cyclist to hold onto, and the back wheel has a little platform each side to kneel on. The cyclist's body is the only connection between the two.

The big advantage of a real bicycle is its solid frame that means the wheels can't move further apart. Going downhill might be a problem for the body-connected bike as the front wheel gathers speed.

SHINE A LIGHT—OUT TO SEA

The first lighthouses were built around 2,250 years ago, using candles or open fires as a source of light.

light

fresnel lens

Then in 1822, the French inventor Augustin Fresnel invented a system of magnifying and reflecting lenses and prisms to focus the light from a lantern into a narrow beam and send it out far over the water. The Fresnel lens, as it became known, was first used in a lighthouse in France. The light was visible 32 km (20 miles) away.

A flame with no reflectors wasted 97 percent of the light, but one with a Fresnel lens focused and used 83 percent of the light. Fresnel's design saved countless lives in avoided shipwrecks.

We hope you don't need one...

...but if you do need an ambulance, you have French surgeon Dominique Jean Larrey to thank.

Upset at the deaths of injured soldiers not picked up from the battlefield during fighting, he adapted a gun carriage to make a wagon that could roll over the wrecked land of a battlefield. He called it a "flying ambulance."

flying ambulance

The first civilian ambulances were introduced in London in 1832 to carry cholera patients. The patients' treatment started en route to the hospital, as it does in a modern ambulance.

TAKE A SNAKE FOR A SLITHER

If you've got a dog, it's pretty easy to take it for a walk. You put a collar around its neck and attach a leash. The dog can't slip through the collar because the bits either side—the head and the body—are thicker than the neck. But what if you have a snake? A snake is pretty much all neck. As the snake moves forward, the collar will just slide down the narrowing body until the snake is gone.

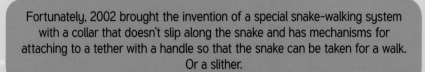

Fortunately, 2002 brought the invention of a special snake-walking system with a collar that doesn't slip along the snake and has mechanisms for attaching to a tether with a handle so that the snake can be taken for a walk. Or a slither.

Just in case dogs feel free to laugh at snakes going for a slither in special non-slip collars, there are equally odd accessories for dogs.

KEEP YOUR EARS OUT OF YOUR FOOD

(if you're a dog).

A dog with long ears like a poodle or spaniel might have problems with its ears draping in its food bowl and getting covered in dog food.

WHAT A FABULOUS IDEA!

Luckily, dogs need not suffer dirty ears. Designed in 1979, these rigid ear protectors close around the ears and hold them out horizontally from the side of the head. A strap around the neck holds the protectors in place. It didn't really catch on.

THEIR TIME HAS COME— AND GONE

Before electronic calculators, people used a slide rule to work out complicated multiplication and division. It looked like a ruler with sliding panels and was invented in **1632**.

Small, electronic, "pocket" calculators appeared in **1970** in Japan. Now everyone uses the calculator app on their phone.

The first telephone directory was a single sheet of paper listing the 50 telephones in New Haven, USA in **1878**.

The floppy disk, once used to store computer files, was invented by Alan Shugart in **1967**. The first disks were 20 cm (8 in) across.

Before PDFs, fax machines sent a picture of a document over the phone lines. The idea dates back to **1864**, but the first modern(ish) commercial fax machine appeared in **1964**.

13-cm (5¼ in) disk

fire steel

flint

Fire steels were invented around **1200 BCE** to light fires. They work by striking metal against flint to make sparks. They were used until the invention of matches.

Gustaf Thulin Sten invented the plastic carrier bag in **1965**. Twenty years later, 75 percent of grocery stores used them. Now they are being phased out and banned as they are so damaging to the environment.

In **1876**, Melville Bissel invented a mechanical carpet sweeper with revolving brushes that swept up dirt into a box. The vacuum cleaner has replaced it.

Trading stamps were invented in **1896** in the USA. Shops and other traders gave customers stamps, which they saved up to claim a reward. They were most popular in the **1960s**.

GRAND RAPIDS

Baby cages were invented in **1922** as a way of giving babies in apartment blocks sunlight and fresh air. The baby lay or sat in the cage, suspended over a huge drop … what could go wrong?

STRIKE A LIGHT

We take it for granted that we can strike a match to light a candle on a birthday cake, or start a camp fire. But until 1805, people could only start a fire with a fire steel or magnifying lens.

The first match, invented by Jean Chancel in France, had a mix of chemicals on a stick that was dipped in acid. The reaction produced so much heat it set fire to the stick. It wasn't very safe, as it produced poisonous gases right next to the user.

The first match to be lit by striking it on a rough surface was invented in England by John Walker in 1826.

STRIKE A LIGHT with a LIGHTER

The lighter was invented before the strikable match. German chemist Johann Wolfgang Döbereiner made the first lighter in 1823. It worked by using a chemical reaction to produce a flammable gas—hydrogen—in a small space and then striking a flint to set light to the gas as it came out of a small hole. It was called Döbereiner's lamp.

Around 20,000 of his "lamps" were sold during his lifetime, but as Döbereiner didn't register the design he made little money from it.

modern lighter

TALKING TO DOLPHINS

It would be great if we could talk to animals, but our bodies aren't shaped to make the right kind of sounds. Never mind—in 1992, film company Walt Disney invented a special keyboard for talking to dolphins.

The keyboard links keys with pictures of objects and makes a sound when a picture is selected. A dolphin can press a key with its snout, or interrupt a beam of light connected with the key, triggering the sound. A person can do the same, so the dolphin and person can talk.

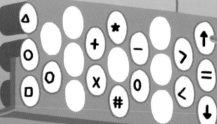

The designers suggested that dolphins could use it to communicate with each other, but it's hard to see why dolphins would do that, since they already all speak dolphin.

STITCHING **LEGS** TOGETHER ...

The first tights were for men. Not for superheroes, but for men in the 1400s.

The legs were baggy, made of woven material, and attached at the top to a pouch called a codpiece that covered the front of the lower body. They weren't properly tights as the legs were separate. They were a long way from the stretchy, clingy, close-fitting, nylon tights of today. In the 1700s, women started to wear stockings, too.

modern tights

nylon stockings

With the invention of nylon in 1935, stockings were transformed. Nylon began to replace silk in 1938. The first tights went on sale in the 1950s. They were made by stitching stockings to thin, stretchy briefs.

AN END TO SOGGY CEREAL

Don't you just hate it when the last bit of cereal in your bowl has turned to soggy mush?

Luckily, in 1990 American Alton Davis invented a special cereal bowl that lets you enjoy crispy cereal to the last mouthful.

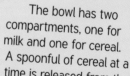

The bowl has two compartments, one for milk and one for cereal. A spoonful of cereal at a time is released from the cereal area and falls down a chute into the milk bowl. You eat that spoonful and trigger another delivery to the milk area.

Reinforced concrete—concrete strengthened with metal rods—was invented in France by **FRANÇOIS COIGNET** in 1853.

STRONGER THAN CONCRETE

He made a house in Paris that used metal bars to stop the tall walls falling over.

Another Frenchman, **JOSEPH MONIER**, improved it a great deal. In 1877 he registered a design for concrete with metal rods arranged in a grid pattern. Monier was a gardener and had started by looking for a way of making stronger flowerpots. He first used a metal mesh in a mortar shell.

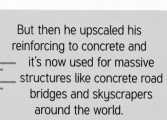

But then he upscaled his reinforcing to concrete and it's now used for massive structures like concrete road bridges and skyscrapers around the world.

271

IT'S A MATERIAL WORLD

Leo Baekland invented the very first plastic in 1907, called **BAKELITE**. It was hard and brittle and usually brown. It made good doorknobs.

GLASS is easy to make by melting sand. It was used in Mesopotamia in the Middle East 4,500 years ago.

NYLON was invented in 1935 by Wallace Carothers. The first nylon object on sale was a toothbrush; the second was stockings.

A form of **CONCRETE** was first used 2,700 years ago. It was used by Arab traders to make, among other things, water cisterns hidden underground in the desert.

POLYSTYRENE was first made accidentally by Eduard Simon in 1839, then largely ignored for nearly 100 years. A German company started making it as a useful plastic in 1931.

Ray McIntire invented polystyrene foam by accident during World War II while trying to make an electrical insulator. **STYROFOAM** products were introduced in 1954.

PARTICLEBOARD, or **CHIPBOARD**, is wood chippings, shavings, or sawdust glued together with resin. It was invented in 1887 in Germany as a wood substitute made from wood dust and glue.

KEVLAR was invented by Stephanie Kwolek in 1965. It's five times stronger than steel and much lighter—perfect for bulletproof vests, spacesuits, and all kinds of protective gear.

The first **BRICKS** were made 10,000 years ago from clay and straw left to bake hard in the sun.

STEEL is much stronger than iron. It's made by mixing a little carbon into molten iron and was first made around 4,000 years ago. A modern process for making steel was invented in the 1850s and drove the American industrial revolution.

THE FIRST BIG BANG

Chinese chemists searching for a medicine that would bring eternal life instead discovered a deadly substance—gunpowder. Around 850 BCE, Chinese chemists found a powder that could produce explosions and flames. It was so dangerous that some scientists burned their hands or even their houses.

It was quickly put to use in tubes attached to arrows, then set alight and fired at Mongolian enemies. The chemists had invented the first explosive weapon and the first firework at the same time. The Chinese army went on to be the first to use canons and grenades, also powered by gunpowder.

AN UNSOLVABLE PUZZLE

Rubik's cube is a three-dimensional puzzle that was invented in 1974 by Hungarian architect Erno Rubik.

Rubik wasn't making a puzzle or a toy. He wanted a model to explain three-dimensional geometry. His cube has faces divided into nine squares, with faces of white, blue, red, yellow, orange, and green. When he turned rows of squares, the faces became jumbled. The more he moved, the more jumbled the cube became until he found he couldn't put it back to how it started. It can be arranged in 43 quintillion (43,000,000,000,000,000,000) different ways.

Rubik launched his "magic cube" as a toy in 1979. It sold hundreds of millions, becoming the bestselling toy of all time.

ANOTHER BIG BANG— IT'S DYNAMITE!

The Swedish chemist Alfred Nobel invented the explosive dynamite in 1867. He made it by mixing nitroglycerin and a soft, powdered mineral that would absorb it. It was intended for blasting rocks apart at quarries and mining sites. In 1876, he made gelatin, a gel-like explosive. Both were successful and he became very wealthy.

Explosives are not always put to good uses, though. When Nobel's brother Ludvig died in 1888, a newspaper mistakenly reported Alfred's death calling him a "merchant of death" because of all the people killed by his inventions. Upset at how he would be remembered, Alfred set up the system of Nobel prizes for great work in science, literature, and promoting peace.

ALFR·
NOBEL

NAT·
MDCCC
XXXIII
OB·
MDCCC
XCVI

Nobel prize medal

AN ALARMING ARM

It's easy to miss a call or message if your phone is on vibrate, even if it's in your pocket. The Finnish phone company Nokia and inventor Zoran Radivojevic came up with a simple solution in 2003—a tattoo that vibrates when your phone rings. It could have different types of vibration for different activities such as calls, messages, and alarms. (It doesn't exist yet—don't rush to the tattooist.)

The tattoo, made of a magnetic material would be tied to your own phone and could be invisible. But what when you get a new phone? How many tattoos would you need over a lifetime?

WHO NEEDS A RAKE?

—when you can wear
leaf-collecting trousers.

They're not quite trousers as they don't have a top part but that's a small quibble when they are saving so much effort.

The "trousers" consist of two separate leg covers or "stalls" which each fasten with a zip to a net strung between them. The idea is to put them on over your other clothes and then walk along through fallen leaves, which are trapped by the net and pushed in front of you into a pile. It sounds as though it might get hard quite quickly.

And who needs a LAWNMOWER?

Mowing the lawn is boring—
ask any grown-up with a lawn.
But riding a tricycle is fun.
So why not combine the two?

Deanna Porath invented just the thing in 1982. It's a tricycle with a set of spinning blades attached to the back so it cuts the grass as you cycle over it.

The tricycle lawnmower is quiet, doesn't use any fuel and because it's good fun people can persuade their children to do the mowing. Small children fall off tricycles pretty often, though, and a set of spinning blades right behind the seat doesn't look like the safest arrangement.

SHOPPING IN A **MALL** WAS SUPPOSED TO BE **FUN**

Victor Gruen

The shopping mall was invented by an Austrian refugee, Victor Gruen, who was saddened by what he saw as the soul-less suburbs around American towns and cities.

The first of his "shopping towns" opened in 1956—Southdale Mall in Edina, Minnesota. He had hoped for bustling cultural hubs with not just stores but places to watch plays and concerts, dotted with sculptures—somewhere lovely and uplifting.

Changes in American tax laws made it possible to build uglier malls without too much risk and the mall soon took a downturn, leaving out the pleasant cultural parts and moving far out of town to the cheapest land. Gruen hated them.

LOUD AND CLEAR

The loudspeaker might seem like a harmless enough invention. It was made by a Danish inventor called Peter Laurids Jensen who moved to the USA in 1909.

Magnavox

Jensen made the "Magnavox" to amplify the voice of a speaker or a recording and gave a demonstration in 1915 by broadcasting Christmas carols in San Francisco. It's hard to imagine the impact of suddenly being able to project a voice further than just by shouting.

Unfortunately, the first politician to take notice of its possibilities was Nazi leader Adolf Hitler. His minister of propaganda, Joseph Goebbels, had loudspeakers set up on street corners around Germany so Hitler's hate-filled speeches could be heard by everyone.

WOULD YOU WEAR A MUZZLE?

Worried by the rise in obesity in America, inventor Lucy Barmby designed an "anti-eating face mask" in 1980.

Fierce dogs are muzzled to stop them biting people or other animals, but this is essentially a person-muzzle to stop people biting anything, but especially food.

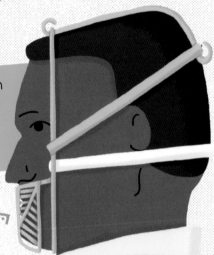

Barmby claimed that constant exposure to the food they were preparing made chefs and "housewives" too liable to snacking and so overeating. What they needed, she thought, was a mask to stop them eating. It covered the mouth but didn't prevent speaking or breathing (phew!). However, it's hard to see how it would be particularly effective, as they could just take it off ...

Let them walk all over you

Do you have a pet gerbil? If so, perhaps you've had to choose between getting the gerbil out to play and letting it run around its tube system.

WOW!

That difficult choice would be removed if the "**GERBIL VEST**" had ever become a success. It was invented in 1999, but you don't see many about.

The gerbil vest contains a network of exciting tubes or tunnels for your gerbils to explore. There are air holes so they can breathe, and the whole thing can be cleaned by flushing through with water (after removing the gerbils). What a great way to carry your pets around with you.

NO NEED FOR BIRD DROPPINGS

Plants need nitrogen to grow well, so we add nitrogen-rich fertilizer to the soil.

In the mid-1800s, bird and bat droppings were a good source of nitrogen fertilizer. Ships sailed to Europe and America from islands off the coast of South America carrying just droppings to use for fertilizer. Later, people also dug nitrogen-rich minerals from Peru.

But the government of Peru took over the mining in 1909 for Peruvian farmers to use the fertilizer, producing a crisis elsewhere. The German chemist Franz Haber solved the problem the same year. He invented the Haber process, which takes nitrogen from the air to make chemicals for fertilizer. There's plenty of air, and not just in Peru!

MAKING ROUND FRUIT AND VEG EASY TO STACK

Round fruit and vegetables are a hassle to package. Luckily, Japanese designer Tomoyuki Ono invented a way of growing watermelons as cubes in 1978.

It's quite easy—they are simply grown inside a box and swell to fill its shape. Although they sell for a lot as novelties, they don't do what she hoped as the melons have to be harvested before they ripen, so they aren't nice to eat.

The melons don't need to be square—they will grow to any shape, including pyramids and love hearts—or even human heads. The "gourd head" is a transparent, head-shaped box invented in 1989 for growing creepy-looking squashes like human heads.

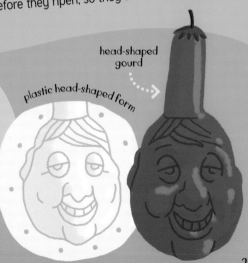

plastic head-shaped form

head-shaped gourd

ACCIDENTS HAPPEN

In 1943, engineer Richard James was trying to design a spring to keep sensitive equipment steady on ships when he knocked over some samples and they "walked" off a shelf. They became the **SLINKY**.

ARTIFICIAL SWEETENERS based on saccharine were invented in 1879 after Constantin Fahlberg forgot to wash his hands before lunch after working with some chemicals. He found his food tasted sweet, and set about making the chemical into a sweetener.

In 1886 American pharmacist John Stith Pemberton was trying to make a painkilling medicine when he came up with **COCA-COLA**.

In 1968, Spencer Silver developed a kind of sticky stuff that he couldn't find a use for. In 1974, Arthur Fry put it to use making **POST-IT NOTES**— originally invented to mark his place in a hymn book.

During World War II, James Wright was trying to make artificial rubber when he accidentally invented **SILLY PUTTY**. It went on sale as a toy in 1950.

PLAY-DOH was invented in 1955 by Joseph and Noah McVicker when they were trying to make a substance to clean wallpaper.

John and Will Kellogg accidentally let some boiled wheat go stale. They tried to roll it into sheets to make dough, but it broke into flakes. They toasted the flakes, making the first **CORNFLAKES** in 1894.

In 1904, a stall selling ice cream at the World's Fair ran out of plates. It rolled up waffles from a nearby stall and put the ice cream in those, inventing the **ICE CREAM CONE**.

The first **MAUVE DYE** was invented when young chemist William Perkin was trying to make a cure for malaria in 1856. His experiment went wrong and made a horrible mess—but a mess that dyed things mauve.

VULCANIZED RUBBER, which can be heated or cooled without spoiling, was invented when Charles Goodyear accidentally spilled a mixture of chemicals and rubber onto a stove.

The **HEART PACEMAKER** was invented in 1956 when Wilson Greatbatch put the wrong resistor in a device he was making to record heartbeats and found it made the heart beat regularly.

287

SKIING UPHILL?

Skiing is great but it needs three things—snow, hills, and energy (yours).

An invention from 1980 can't get round the need for snow, but it does make it easy to ski without hills to go down and without using too much of your energy.

The uphill skier has an engine and a rotor to propel you forward when gravity can't pull you along—because you are going uphill or over flat ground. The rotor is worn as a backpack and has handles that extend around the side to make steering easy.

CARRY THAT COW!

You must have had days when having your hands full of the cow you are carrying has been a real inconvenience. No? Then perhaps you don't need the special, hands-free, calf-carrying harness invented in 1992.

When calves are newborn out in a field they can get chilly, so farmers often need to carry them to a snug barn. But cows are big animals and even a calf gets heavy. This calf-carrier makes it easier, and—the inventor claimed—can be used while riding a horse or driving a tractor.

STICK WITH NON-STICK

In 1938, American chemist Roy J. Plunkett was experimenting with chemicals to use in refrigerators. Working with cylinders of a gas, he discovered that one contained no gas, but weighed the same as when it was full. He cut it open and found a slithery white powder had formed inside that didn't change at high temperatures. It was soon developed into **TEFLON**, now used in everything from pans to spacecraft.

The idea for non-stick pans came more than 10 years later. At a banquet to celebrate Plunkett's invention, all guests had a non-stick pan to take home. Teflon bakeware then took kitchens by storm.

GIVE YOUR TONGUE AN EASY LIFE

Have you ever resented the effort it takes to turn an ice cream cone around as you eat it? Or the hard work of moving your tongue? Would you prefer just to keep your tongue in one place and have the ice cream delivered to it automatically?

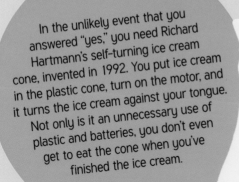

In the unlikely event that you answered "yes," you need Richard Hartmann's self-turning ice cream cone, invented in 1992. You put ice cream in the plastic cone, turn on the motor, and it turns the ice cream against your tongue. Not only is it an unnecessary use of plastic and batteries, you don't even get to eat the cone when you've finished the ice cream.

KNOW WHERE YOU ARE

The magnetic compass was invented in China 2,000 years ago. A magnetized iron object naturally lines up along Earth's north–south magnetic field. The first compasses were "lodestones," naturally magnetized iron stones. Made into a spoon shape, they would line up with the "handle" pointing south.

lodestone

Later compasses used a magnetized needle floating in water or suspended.

The compass revolutionized travel. Before, people had navigated by the stars, which is fine on a clear night but not during daylight, or when it's cloudy.

The compass came to Europe around 800 years ago. With a compass, sailors could cross the oceans for the first time rather than sailing around the edges. It opened up the world for discovery and trade—and also bad things, like invasions and slavery.

French chemist Édouard Bénédictus was standing on a ladder in 1903 when he knocked a glass flask onto the floor. It smashed, but kept its shape, with all the pieces still in place. The flask had contained a kind of liquid plastic that had evaporated but left a thin film stuck to the surface that held the pieces together.

SAFETY FIRST!

The same week, Bénédictus read about people being horribly injured by flying glass from car windshields in accidents. He spent the next 24 hours experimenting and by the end of the next day had invented safety glass. It was used for glass in car windows from 1919, saving countless lives.

ECHO LOCATION WITHOUT BATS

Radar works by bouncing radio waves off an object and monitoring the echo as they come back, showing how far away the object is.

Telemobiloscope

The German physicist Heinrich Hertz showed in the late 1880s that metal objects reflect radio. In 1904, Christian Hülsmeyer first demonstrated his "Telemobiloscope," showing it could detect an iron gate hidden behind a curtain. Hülsmeyer's invention was intended to avoid collisions at sea between metal ships (not collisions with gates hidden behind a curtain).

During World War II, several countries secretly and independently developed radar systems capable of spotting enemy ships and aircraft. Radar operators noticed how rain, sleet, and snow interfered with radar and later developed it for tracking weather.

DEATH TO BUGS— and everything else

The chemical DDT was invented in 1873 but largely ignored until 1939 when the Swiss chemist Paul Muller noticed how readily it kills bugs. It was soon used to kill disease-carrying insects in tropical places. If it had just been used for that, it would probably have been fine.

But after World War II, the US government encouraged farmers to spray DDT on fields to protect crops from insect damage.

DDT quickly went right through the food chain, killing not just harmful insects but useful ones, and birds, fish, reptiles, and anything else that ate insects or came into contact with the chemical on plants and in rivers. It was banned in the USA in 1972.

LET THE SUN SHINE ...

The French scientist Edmond Becquerel realized we could get useful electricity from sunlight in 1839. It turned out to be rather hard to do, though.

In 1883, Charles Fritts installed the first solar panels on a rooftop in New York, but they only converted one percent of the energy they received from the Sun to electricity. A long period of designing and experimenting followed until the first, tiny, working solar cells went on sale in 1956. They were very expensive and only worked with low-power objects such as toys and radios.

The first solar power station was built in California in 1982. Solar power could be a world-saving source of energy in the fight against climate change.

... OR LET THE WIND BLOW

The first windmills were probably built in Persia (now Iran) about 1,200 years ago. Unlike later vertical windmills, they were horizontal, with 6–12 blades made of reed matting or cloth turning a vertical shaft. They were used to grind grain to make flour or to draw water from a well.

Vertical windmills appeared in northwest Europe 800–900 years ago. Like horizontal windmills, they were mechanical. They converted the movement of the blades to a different, useful movement.

Windmills are now used to generate "clean" electricity, and are called wind turbines. The first wind turbine was made in 1887 in Scotland—a very windy place.

WHEELING OUT THE TRASH

The modern dumpster was invented in 1936 in Tennessee, USA. The first variations were specifically designed to fit onto a hoist fitted to the back of a truck for easy emptying.

It wasn't until the 1980s that local authorities gave them to households and businesses, making the job of collecting waste safer and easier.

Why did it take so long to invent? It's a pretty obvious idea. Maybe it didn't— there might have been wooden wheelie bins in the Roman town of Pompeii nearly 2,000 years ago. Fragments of what seems to be a wooden waste crate on wheels have been dug up there.

Pompeii

TREADMILLS MAKE YOU FIT— but they're a PUNISHING regime

People use a treadmill at the gym to go running without going outside in all weathers. It can seem tough, unrewarding, and boring—and that's just what it was intended to be.

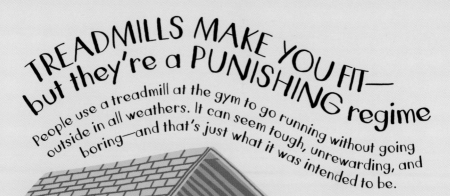

The original treadmill was invented in 1818 by William Cubitt as a way of putting prisoners to good use while punishing them. Groups of prisoners stepped around a paddlewheel, like an everlasting staircase, turning a shaft that then powered machinery such as a mill or water pump. It was far worse than a gym; they had to do 6 hours every day on the machine.

The treadmill was revived as a running machine in 1952 and became popular in gyms in the 1970s.

THAT IS **NOT** A GOOD IDEA

In **1882**, Samuel Applegate invented "an improved device for waking persons from sleep." It was an alarm clock that hit people on the head with lots of little blocks of wood.

In **1979**, Pat Vidas invented a trumpet that blew out flames. It ignited gas from a concealed cylinder to add a bit of drama to the music.

The first glow-in-the-dark clocks appeared around **1917**. The women who painted the numbers licked their paintbrushes and were poisoned by the radioactive radium paint they were using.

The crinoline was a steel-hooped petticoat invented in France in **1856** to make women's dresses stand out. It made it difficult to go through doors or do anything else normal.

ARSENIC

Bright green dye for clothes was invented in **1817** in Germany. Unfortunately, it was made from a very poisonous chemical called arsenic, which causes skin ulcers and hair loss.

Several types of "diet water" were introduced in Japan in **2004**. These bottled waters have no calories. But all water has no calories.

Leaded gasoline (petrol) was invented in **1921** by Thomas Midgley to prevent problems in fuel tanks, but lead is a poison. Pumping it into the air was a bad idea. It was phased out in the 1980s.

Midgley also invented Freon, a chemical used in fridges. It made a hole in the protective ozone layer of Earth's atmosphere.

Gary Thuerk invented junk email messages (spam) in **1975**, sending an unsolicited advertising message to hundreds of computer users.

SPAM

Smell-O-Vision was launched and died in **1960**. A system for releasing smells in time with crucial points in a movie, it was used with only one movie ever.

Bots made spam far worse. Invented in **1997**, they can send thousands of emails at a time.

Hindenburg

The first airships were filled with hydrogen, which burns easily. In **1937** the airship Hindenberg burst into flames. Hydrogen-filled airships quickly went out of fashion.

INDEX